ACE YOUR MICROECONOMICS

WITH MODEL EXPLANATIONS AND EVALUATIONS

Kelvin Hong

Marissa Chok

i

First Printing: 2015

ISBN 978-981-09-5474-1

Edventures Pte Ltd

Singapore

www.TheEconomicsTutor.com

Acknowledgments

This work would not have been possible without the help of Samuel Tay and Lim Wei Jie who provided valuable inputs and helped in reviewing and editing the work.

PREFACE

This book addresses many possible questions across the entire Microeconomics syllabus and was created to provide students with top quality explanations, diagrams, examples, evaluations, insights and expert tips to excel in their examinations.

Very often, students are unable to provide step-by-step explanations and relevant evaluation points, which are essential to scoring in examinations.

By studying the explanations provided in this book, students will also be able to better understand the various economic concepts covered in the Microeconomics syllabus. The powerful diagrammatic analyses provided will also train students to illustrate economic concepts logically, and enable them to use such diagrams for analyses in a more effective and concise manner.

Expert tips have also been added to help the students better remember, understand and apply significant concepts, as well as avoid common errors and misconceptions.

We hope that this book will help all readers better appreciate what they are learning and excel in their Microeconomics examinations.

Kelvin Hong
Marissa Chok

CONTENTS

1. Explain why Supply is upward sloping.

The supply curve represents the quantity of goods and services which producers are **willing** and **able** to sell **at each price level**, during a given time period.

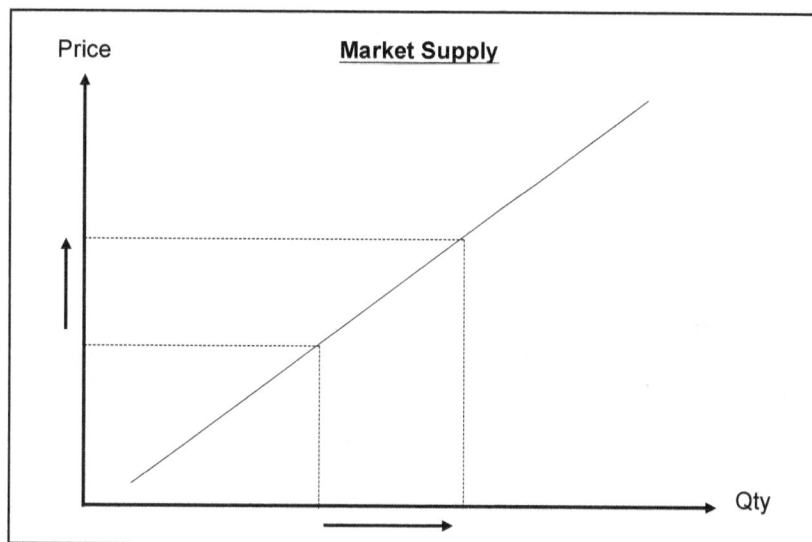

The Law of Supply dictates that there is a positive relationship between price and quantity supplied (Qs). This means that as price increases, Qs will increase, and as price decreases, Qs will decrease.

When price increases, profit-motivated producers have greater incentive to increase the quantity supplied of the good because the **higher marginal cost of supplying an additional unit** can be covered by the higher **marginal benefit** of the **additional revenue** earned from the sale of the good at a higher price.

A. Increasing Marginal Cost
As producers increase the quantity supplied of a certain good, they will incur a higher marginal cost of production. In order to cover this cost, producers will have to increase the price of their good.

<u>Law of Diminishing Marginal Returns</u>
In the **short run**, as more units of a variable factor (e.g. labour) are applied to a given quantity of a fixed factor (e.g. machine), there comes a point beyond which **extra** output from the additional unit of the variable factor will eventually diminish. Thus, **marginal cost** will rise as **marginal product** will eventually decrease when the quantity of variable factor increases in order to increase quantity supplied.

<u>Law of Increasing Costs of Production</u>
In addition, as producers increase the quantity supplied of a particular good, they will incur increasing marginal costs as the factors of production which must be used

to produce greater quantities of that good are **increasingly less suitable and/or productive.** This is because the most suitable factors were already hired earlier. Thus, **marginal costs** will rise while **marginal product** will eventually decrease, requiring a **need to receive a higher price** in order to increase quantity supplied.

B. Greater Profit Margins

Furthermore, as price increases, there is **greater incentive** to devote resources to produce this good as **profit margins increase.** Thus, producers may now direct resources from the production of other goods to this good, increasing the quantity supplied.

Evaluation:

Price Elasticity of Supply

The gradient of the Supply curve is dependent on its Price Elasticity of Supply (PES), which is a measure of the responsiveness of quantity supplied to changes in price, ceteris paribus. The more elastic the supply, the gentler the gradient of the supply curve.

Tip

In economics, the word "marginal" carries the same meaning as "extra" or "change".

2. Explain competitive supply.

When two goods are in competitive supply, this means that **both goods compete for the use of the same factor inputs or resources**, such that producing more of one good would mean **diverting resources away** from the production of the other good.

For example, a farmer can choose to produce maize for biofuel or for consumption. An increase in the demand for maize for consumption would create a **shortage of maize** in this market, creating an upward pressure on price as consumers bid up the price of maize. As prices increase, producers increase quantity supplied (Qs) to enjoy greater profitability, while consumers decrease quantity demanded (Qd). This occurs until the new equilibrium is reached at Q1, where the shortage is eliminated and the price of maize as food has increased from P0 to P1.

As a result of increasing the Qs of maize for food, the supply of Biofuel decreases, leading to a leftward shift of the supply curve from S0 to S1.

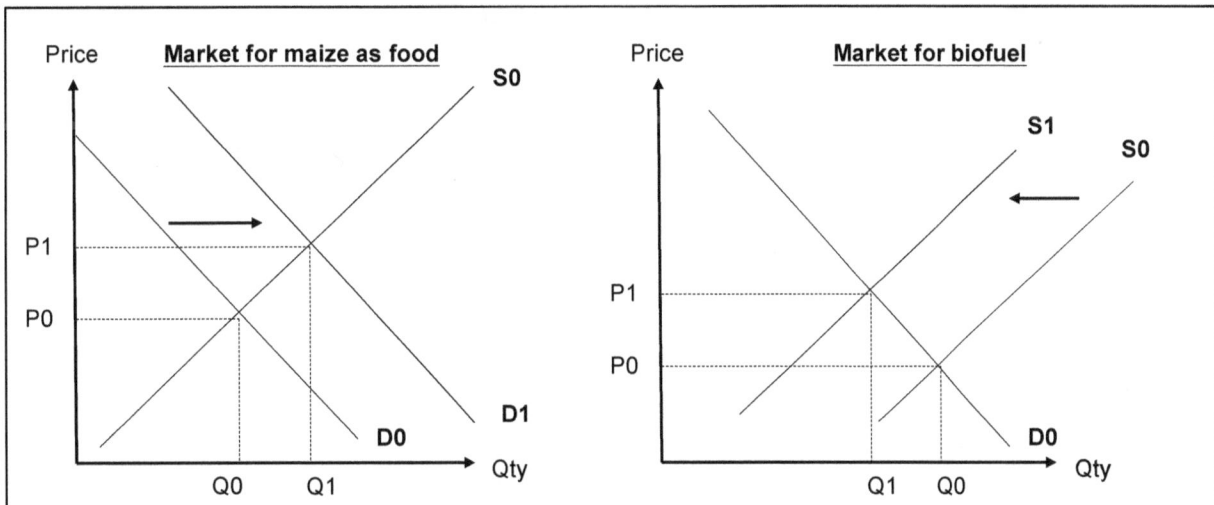

Evaluation:

In the long term, the farmers can choose to invest in more land, better quality seeds, technology and so on, thereby increasing supply of **both** maize for food and maize for biofuel.

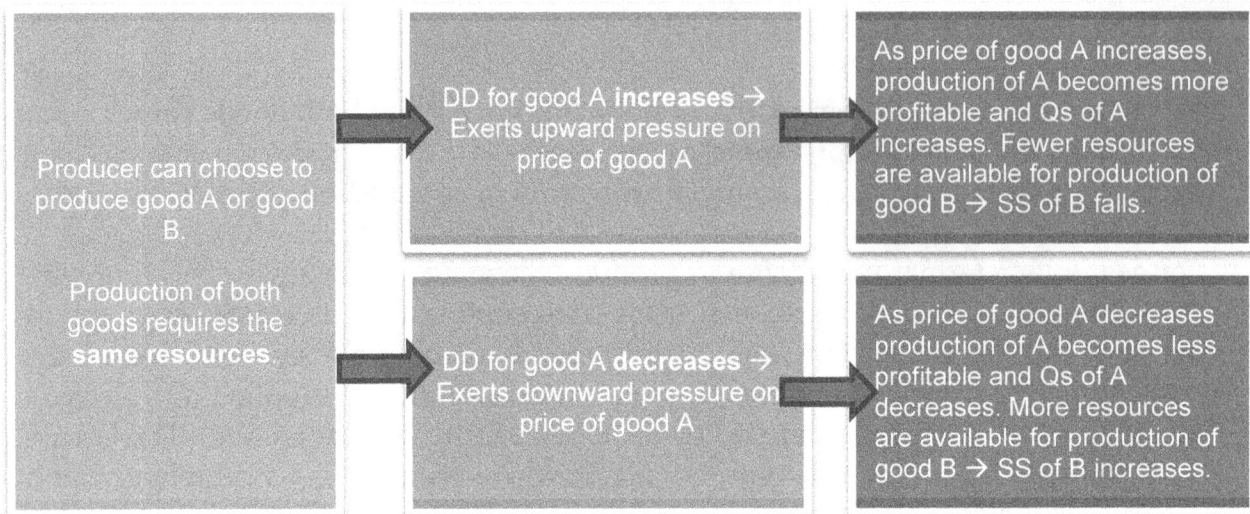

Producer can choose to produce good A or good B.

Production of both goods requires the **same resources**.

DD for good A **increases** → Exerts upward pressure on price of good A

As price of good A increases, production of A becomes more profitable and Qs of A increases. Fewer resources are available for production of good B → SS of B falls.

DD for good A **decreases** → Exerts downward pressure on price of good A

As price of good A decreases production of A becomes less profitable and Qs of A decreases. More resources are available for production of good B → SS of B increases.

3. Explain how expectations may affect demand and supply.

<u>Expectations of Price Increase/Decrease (Inflationary and Deflationary expectations)</u>
If **prices of a particular good are expected to increase**, consumers may **increase their demand** for this good in the present, so as to avoid paying higher prices in the future.

Conversely, if **producers anticipate that the prices of their goods will increase**, they may **reduce market supply** and hoard their stocks of the good, with the intention of only releasing them into the market when price increases. This is so as to earn higher revenues.

<u>Expectations of Income Changes</u>
If consumers expect their incomes to increase, their demand for goods (assuming these are **normal goods**) will **increase** as they believe their purchasing power has increased and thus, their current expenditure will increase even if incomes have not yet increased. Likewise, if a consumer expects incomes to decrease, demand for goods and services will fall as consumers lower their current expenditure.

Evaluation:

<u>Self-fulfilling expectations</u>
Consumer expectations can become **self-fulfilling** when their expectations influence their behaviour in a manner which causes their expectations to be realised. For example, if consumers and producers expect prices to increase, this will cause **demand to increase** and **supply to fall** such that **price does indeed increase**.

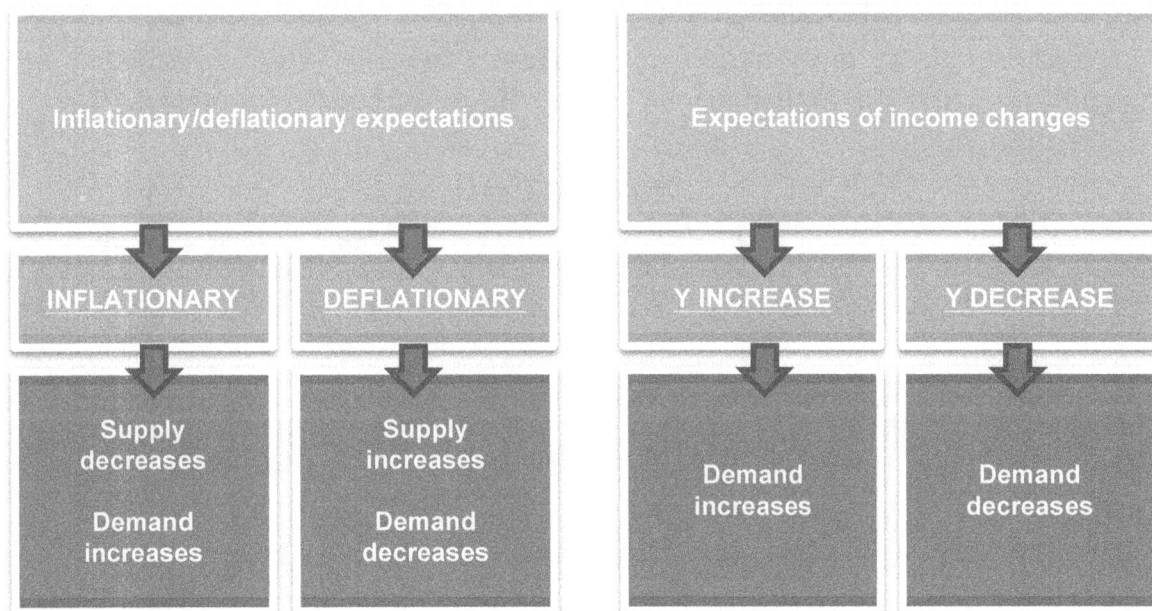

Inflationary/deflationary expectations		Expectations of income changes	
INFLATIONARY	DEFLATIONARY	Y INCREASE	Y DECREASE
Supply decreases Demand increases	Supply increases Demand decreases	Demand increases	Demand decreases

4. Explain how the Price Mechanism allocates resources.

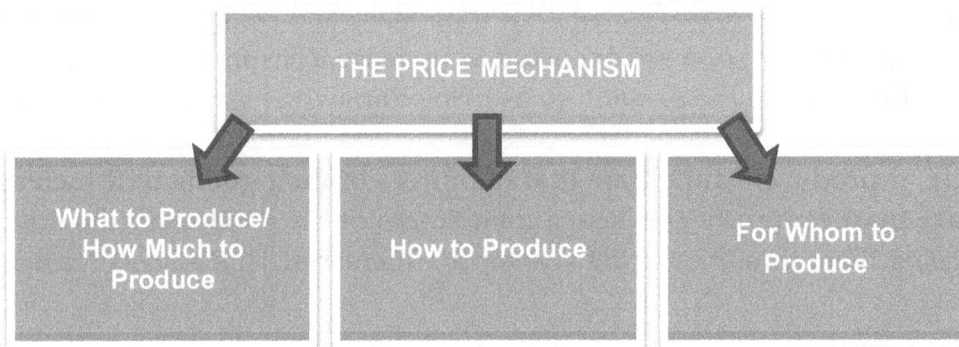

THE PRICE MECHANISM

What to Produce/ How Much to Produce | How to Produce | For Whom to Produce

The Price Mechanism refers to the free market forces of demand and supply which help to determine the market equilibrium price and quantity of a good. It serves as a **signal, incentive and rationing tool** which allocates scarce resources by answering the three basic economic questions of a) What to produce and in what quantity, b) How to produce, and c) For whom to produce.

<u>What to produce and how much to produce</u>
Prices serve as **signals** by which producers can accurately gauge the level of demand for their good and thus allocate resources accordingly. For example, an increase in the demand for shoes would lead to a shortage, exerting an **upward pressure** on price. This is because consumers who are unable to obtain the good would **bid up prices** of the good in order to obtain it. The higher prices will be a **signal to the producers that there is a shortage in the market**. In addition, as prices increase, profit margins increase and producing more output becomes **more profitable** and therefore producers will have **greater incentive** to increase the Qs of shoes, leading to more resources being allocated to shoe production. Qs will increase and Qd will decrease until the **new market equilibrium where Qs=Qd** is reached. The new equilibrium quantity exchanged is Q1 while the new equilibrium price is P1.

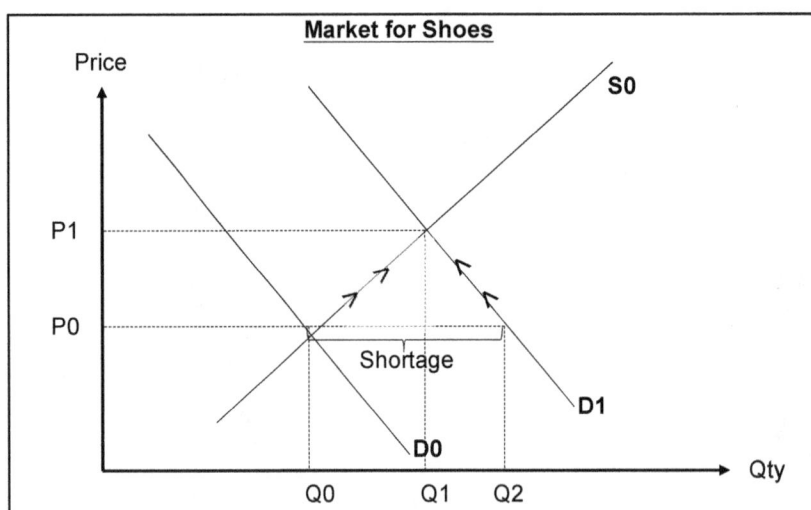

6

Thus, the price mechanism serves to accurately transmit consumers' preferences to producers, and enables the subsequent reallocation of resources to meet the new level of demand.

How to produce

In order to maximise profits (TR-TC), firms aim to increase revenue and reduce cost. Hence, producers are likely to use the least cost methods of production, which is in turn dependent on the prices of factor inputs. Firms will be encouraged to employ factors of production, which it can acquire at the lowest cost. For example, in Singapore, where wages are increasing faster than the prices of capital goods, firms will use more capital-intensive methods to produce, and hence fewer labour resources will be allocated to those industries that can switch to more capital-intensive production.

For whom to produce

The question of 'for whom to produce' is determined by consumers' dollar votes. When quantity demanded exceeds quantity supplied, prices serve as a **rationing tool** that allocates goods and services to consumers, based on their willingness and ability to pay for the good. For example, as shown in the preceding diagram, as prices increase due to the shortage (Q2-Q0), the increase in price helps to ration the limited quantity supplied, as consumers who are unwilling or unable to pay the higher price will no longer demand for the good. Hence Q1Q2 units are no longer demanded for as prices rise from P0 to P1. The goods will only be allocated to those who continue to be willing and able to pay for the good at higher prices, as expressed through their dollar votes.

Evaluation:

In the absence of market failure, such as externalities, the free market achieves **allocative efficiency**, which means it achieves an allocation of scarce resources that maximizes societal welfare, that is, where **Social Surplus (Consumer Surplus + Producer Surplus)** is maximized.

However, in reality, many sources of market failure exist. **As a result, the free market does not necessarily achieve allocative efficiency.**

5. Explain why demand may be price elastic.

The price elasticity of demand (PED) is a measure of the responsiveness of the quantity demanded of a good to changes in the good's own price, ceteris paribus. The more price-elastic the demand for the good, the greater the change in quantity demanded when the good's own price changes.

$$\text{Formula: PED} = \frac{\%\ change\ in\ quantity\ demanded}{\%\ change\ in\ price} = \frac{\Delta Q}{\Delta P} \times \frac{P0}{Q0}$$

PED is influenced by four key factors: The substitutability of the good, the necessity of the good, the proportion of income spent on the good, and the time period over which consumers can adjust to price changes.

Substitutability
The **greater the number of substitutes available**, the **more price-elastic** the demand for the good. For example, there are only a few reputable word-processing softwares available. Thus, the demand for word-processing softwares would be relatively price-inelastic as compared to demand for note-taking mobile applications, for which there are a huge number of substitutes available.

The substitutability of a good is dependent on the **definition of the good**; the broader the definition of the good, the fewer the number of substitutes. For example, if a good is broadly defined as 'food', fewer substitutes will be available and demand will be more price-inelastic. On the other hand, if it is defined (in a narrower sense) as 'beef', for example, substitutes such as chicken, pork, and venison become available and demand will be more price-elastic.

Necessity of a good
If a good is **deemed a necessity and/or habitually consumed**, demand for the good will be **more price-inelastic**. Food, for example, is essential for survival and its demand is thus price-inelastic.

On the other hand, non-essential items such as luxury handbags and watches tend to have more price-elastic demand. The necessity of a good **may vary to different groups of people**. For example, drug addicts may perceive drugs to be of absolute necessity, thus demand for drugs is likely to be more price-inelastic for this group of people.

Proportion of income spent on the good
The **higher the proportion of income spent on a good**, the more consumers would be forced to cut back on consumption when the price of the good increases. Thus, demand for expensive luxury items tends to be **more price-elastic**, in addition to the fact that they are non-essential.

However, note that the proportion of income spent on a particular good can vary across different groups of consumers. For example, purchasing a television may take up a large proportion of an ordinary citizen's income, whereas it takes up a considerably smaller proportion of a wealthy man's income; as such, demand for the television is deemed more price-inelastic for higher-income groups than for lower-income groups.

Time period
Consumers need time to respond to changes in price by changing their consumption patterns and finding new substitutes. The **longer the time period**, the **more price-elastic** the demand, since they have more time to adjust their consumption patterns and find suitable substitutes.

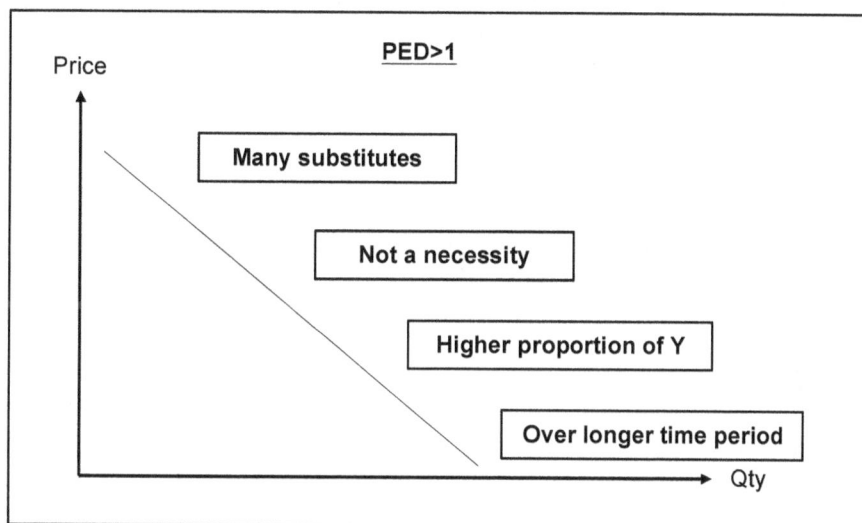

Evaluation:

Pricing strategy
Knowledge of PED values can be useful for a firm in determining pricing strategies to increase revenue. More information on this can be found in **Question 12**.

Gradient of demand curve
PED>1 can be represented by a **gently sloping demand curve**. The curve covers a broad range of quantities, which is consistent with a quantity demanded being highly responsive. In contrast, **PED<1** is represented by a demand curve with a **steep gradient** that covers a smaller range of quantities.

6. Explain why supply may be price-inelastic.

Price elasticity of supply (PES) refers to the **responsiveness of the quantity supplied of a good in response to changes in the good's own price, ceteris paribus.**

$$\text{Formula: PES} = \frac{\% \text{ change in quantity supplied}}{\% \text{ change in price}} = \frac{\Delta Q}{\Delta P} \times \frac{P0}{Q0}$$

Price-elastic supply means that changes in the price of a good will lead to a more than proportionate change in quantity supplied of the good, ceteris paribus. For example, if prices increase, profit-motivated producers would be readily able to increase production by utilising available stocks or devoting more factor inputs to the production of the good. Conversely, price-inelastic supply means that changes in the price of a good would lead to a less than proportionate change in quantity supplied of the good, ceteris paribus.

PES is dependent on the number of firms producing the good, the length and complexity of the production process, the availability of stocks and spare capacity, the time period over which firms can respond to price changes, and degree of factor mobility and substitutability.

Number of firms producing the good
The fewer the number of firms in the industry producing a certain good, the more price-inelastic the supply of that good. This is because for any given change in price, fewer firms will be responding with changes to their Qs, and therefore Qs will be less responsive to the change in price. For example, due to more stringent regulations, the number of private educational institutions in Singapore has dwindled in recent years, causing the supply of educational services to become more price-inelastic over the years.

Length and complexity of production process
The longer and more complex the production process, the more price-inelastic the supply of that good. This is typically the case for **primary products.** For example, the process of growing **agricultural produce** is lengthy as there is a minimum time required before crops can be harvested, time is given to allow the land to lie fallow, and so on. The process of **producing oil** can be complex as it requires highly technical knowledge to plan, drill and complete an oil well. On the other hand, the length of production for **manufactured products** is relatively shorter and with mechanization, manufacturing processes are increasingly less tedious and complex. Thus, the supply of agricultural products tends to be more price-inelastic than the supply of manufactured goods.

Availability of stocks and spare capacity
The **harder it is to store the goods**, and the **smaller the amount of spare capacity** in production, the more price-inelastic the supply because it is difficult to increase and

decrease quantity supplied in response to price changes. For example, a 20-seat diner experiences a more price-inelastic supply because it lacks spare capacity to increase quantity supplied during festive occasions. Similarly, it may be difficult to retain stocks of fresh meat and vegetables due to its perishability thus the supply of these goods would be more price-inelastic in nature.

Time Period/Duration

Supply tends to be more price-inelastic when firms **have less time to adjust their resources/quantity supplied in response to price changes**. For example, in the immediate term, a fisherman's supply of fishes is fixed. In the long run, however, a fisherman can buy better fishing equipment such as larger fishing nets, increase the size or number of his boats, and discover new fishing locations. This allows the supply of fishes to become more price-elastic over time.

Degree of Factor Mobility and Substitutability

Factor mobility is defined as the **ease and speed** at which firms can shift resources from one use to another. The **longer and more difficult** it is for resources to be shifted from one industry to another, the **more price-inelastic the supply of the good**. For example, the supply of healthcare is price-inelastic as it is difficult and takes a long time to convert labour inputs from other industries to become qualified healthcare workers. It is also difficult to substitute these workers with capital goods such as machines.

Evaluation:

Government Policies

In some instances, the government may put in place policies to limit the supply of a certain good, such that the supply of the good becomes **perfectly price-inelastic.** An example would be capping the supply of Certificates of Entitlement (COEs) in Singapore, which causes the supply of new cars to become perfectly price-inelastic at the maximum amount of COEs available as shown in the diagram below. This means that there will be **no change in quantity supplied** in response to a change in price.

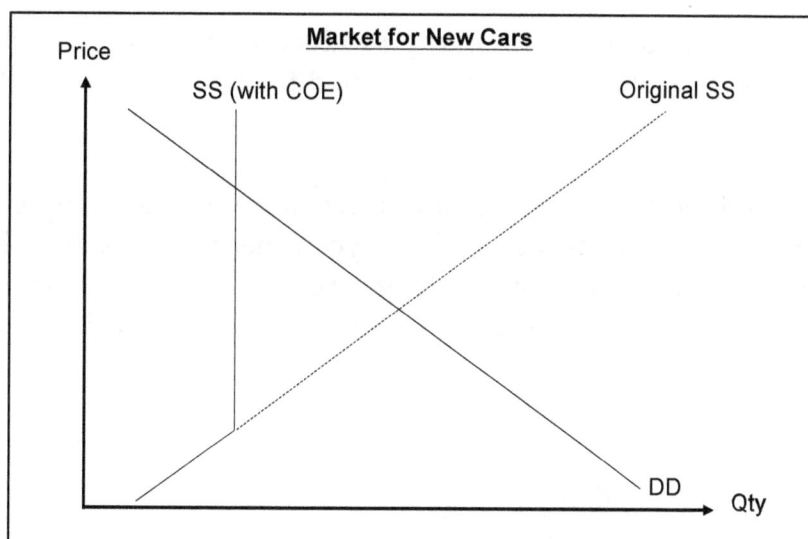

11

7. Explain why supply and demand will be more price-elastic if observing over a longer time horizon.

Demand

In the short run, it may be difficult for consumers to **change their consumption patterns** and **find substitutes** for existing products. As such, they may find it difficult to adjust quantity demanded when price changes occur and demand tends to be price-inelastic. Over a longer time horizon, however, consumers will be able to **shift their consumption patterns and seek viable alternatives for the goods they wish to consume**. As more substitutes become available, demand becomes more price-elastic.

For example, in the short run, demand for car usage may be price-inelastic; in the long run, however, demand for car usage becomes more price-elastic as consumers get used to other forms of transport such as MRT. Thus, if we observe the immediate impact of an increase in toll charges, we will find that consumers are more unresponsive and quantity demanded will fall less than proportionately. However, over a longer time horizon, quantity demanded may fall more than proportionately as more consumers switch to other forms of transportation.

Supply

In the short run, production is constrained by **at least one fixed factor of production** and it is difficult for firms to adjust quantity supplied when price-changes occur. But in the long run, firms will have a **greater amount of time to adjust their factor inputs** and quantity supplied in response to price changes. As such, supply becomes more price-elastic.

For example, in the short run, restaurants may be unable to hire sufficient labour at a reasonable wage to increase quantity supplied. However, in the long run, substitutes such as an iPad ordering system may become available due to technological improvements, enabling the restaurant to expand without having to hire more waitresses.

In addition, certain goods have a **lengthy production period**. As such, in the short run, it may not be possible for quantity supplied to change significantly in response to price changes.

For example, building new housing can take many years to complete. If we view supply over a short period, such as within a year, there is unlikely to be any change in quantity supplied. However, over a longer period, quantity supplied can change more significantly when price changes occur and supply will become more price-elastic.

8. Explain how the relative values of PED and PES will affect the share of government subsidy among producers and consumers.

A subsidy is defined as a **payment made by the government to the producer or consumer**. An indirect subsidy **lowers the cost of production**, thereby shifting the supply curve downwards by the amount of the subsidy and enabling firms to increase output. While the **impact of an indirect subsidy first falls on the producer**, the **benefit** of the subsidy is usually **shared** between the producers and consumers, as producers are able to pass on some of the cost savings to consumers in the form of lowered prices and in return achieve more sales.

The more price-inelastic side of the market generally has more to gain from the indirect subsidy. This means that when **supply is price-inelastic relative to demand, producers are able to benefit more from the subsidy** since they are unlikely to be able to produce a lot more at each and every price level and thus, the excess supply at the initial price will be lesser. On the other hand, consumers do not require much lower prices to increase their quantity demanded. Consequently, the decrease in market price is less, which means that producers do not pass on as much of the cost savings to the consumers, and enjoy the bulk of the benefit from the subsidy.

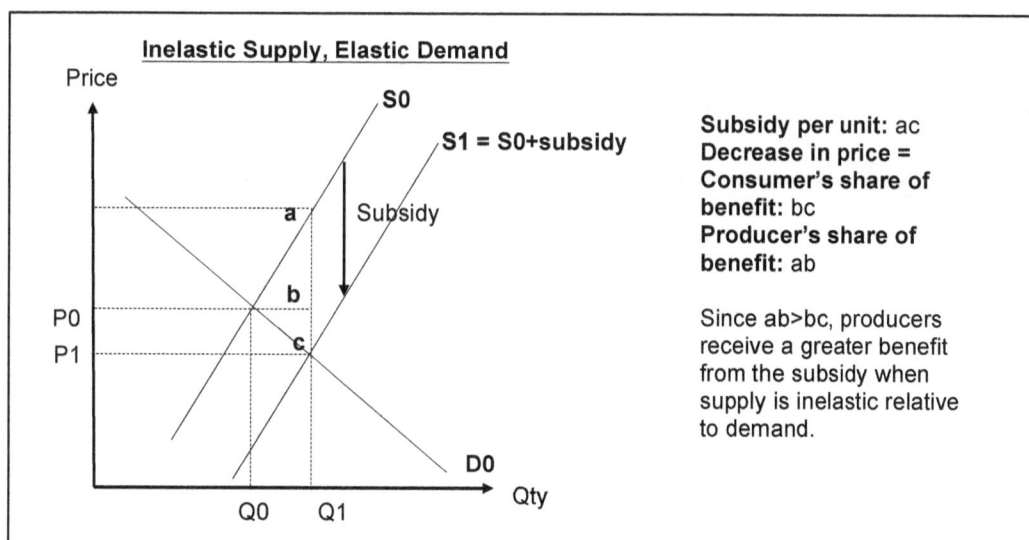

Inelastic Supply, Elastic Demand

Subsidy per unit: ac
Decrease in price = Consumer's share of benefit: bc
Producer's share of benefit: ab

Since ab>bc, producers receive a greater benefit from the subsidy when supply is inelastic relative to demand.

When demand is price-inelastic relative to supply, consumers will receive a greater share of the subsidy as prices will have to be lowered by a greater extent to encourage an increase in quantity demanded. Conversely, producers will benefit less as they are able to produce a lot more at each and every price level and thus, excess supply at the initial price level will be greater. In order to clear their stocks, producers will have to pass on most of the cost savings to the consumers who will enjoy a greater benefit from the subsidy.

Elastic Supply, Inelastic Demand

Price

a

S0

Subsidy

P0 — b

S1 = S0+subsidy

c

P1

D0

Qty

Q0 Q1

Subsidy per unit: ac
Decrease in price =
Consumer's share of
benefit: bc
Producer's share of
benefit: ab

Since bc>ab, consumers
receive a greater benefit
from the subsidy when
demand is inelastic
relative to supply.

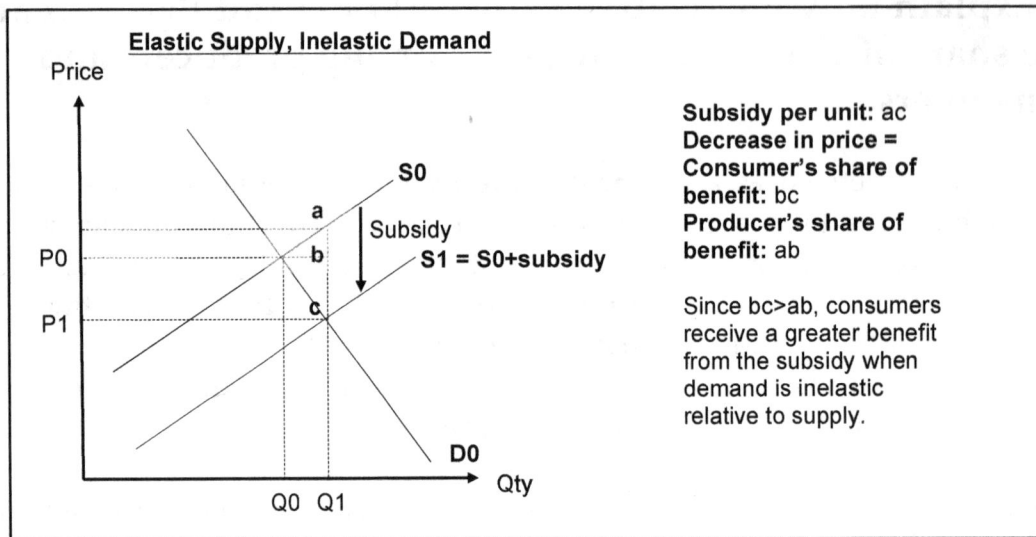

Rather than the absolute levels of PED and PES, it is their **relative values,** which determine the share of the subsidy amongst producers and consumers.

Tip

As a general rule, the more inelastic side of the market will be more affected by the subsidy. The same rule applies to **indirect taxes**.

9. Explain the difference between direct taxes and indirect taxes.

A tax is a **compulsory payment levied on producers or consumers by the government**. For direct taxes, the liability - or 'incidence' - of the tax **cannot be passed on to another individual**, and must be paid directly by the taxpayer. However, although the impact of an indirect tax falls on the producer, the incidence of the tax can be distributed between producers and consumers, as producers can choose to pass on the increase in costs to the consumer through higher prices. **Thus, for indirect taxes, the payer of the tax need not necessarily be the bearer of the tax burden.**

As can be seen from the diagram below, the imposition of a direct tax (such as an income tax) will cause consumers' purchasing power to fall, causing the demand curve to shift leftward from D0 to D1. There is no change in supply. On the other hand, the imposition of an indirect tax per unit causes the supply curve to shift upward from S0 to S1 which is S0+tax. However, although the impact of the tax falls on the producer, the producer is able to pass on some of the the incidence of the tax to the consumer. As shown in the diagram, when a tax per unit equivalent to ac is imposed on the producer, price increases from P0 to P1. Thus, producers bear the tax burden bc, while consumers bear the tax burden of ab which is the increase in price.

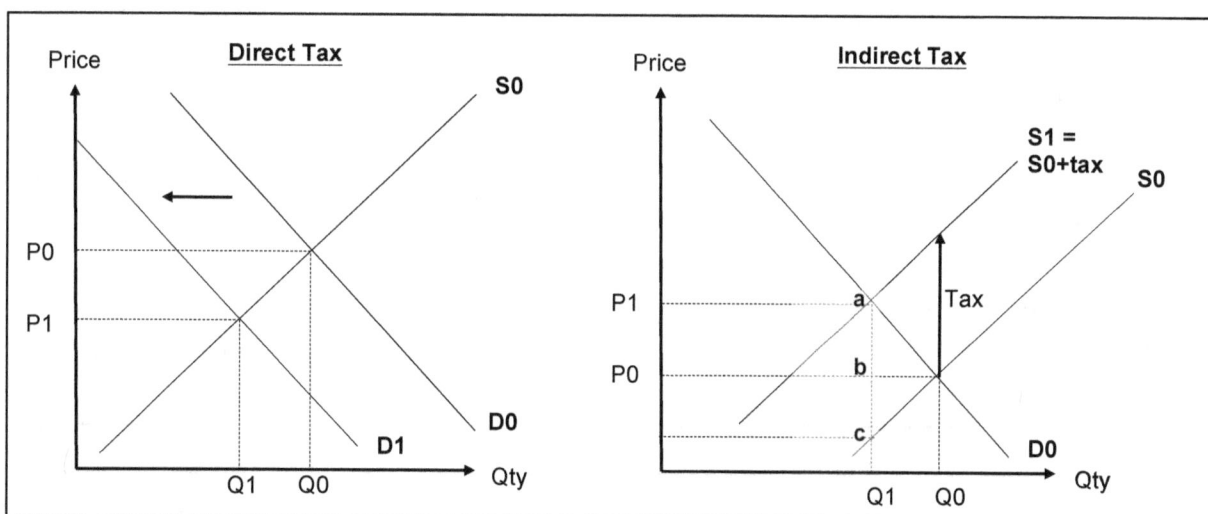

An example of direct tax is **personal income tax**, while examples of indirect taxes include the **Goods and Services Tax (GST), excise taxes on cigarettes** etc.

10. Explain why a Perfectly Competitive firm faces a horizontal demand curve but Monopolistically Competitive firms can face a downward-sloping demand curve.

PC firm

In a perfectly competitive market, there is a **large number of buyers and sellers** and each producer sells **homogeneous** products, which are identical to those of their rivals. As such, rivals' goods are **perfect substitutes** for their products, which translates into a **perfectly price-elastic (horizontal) demand curve** at the prevailing market price.

Since buyers show no preference for the product of any one firm, the firm is a **price taker** and has no control over its price. Individual **firms must sell at the prevailing market price** determined by market forces of demand and supply. If the firm sells its good above the market price, consumers would simply purchase the good from another firm and quantity demanded for the firm's product would fall to zero. Likewise, the firm has no incentive to reduce its price below the market equilibrium price, since it can sell all it wants at the prevailing price.

Thus, a PC firm faces a horizontal demand curve as shown in the diagram below.

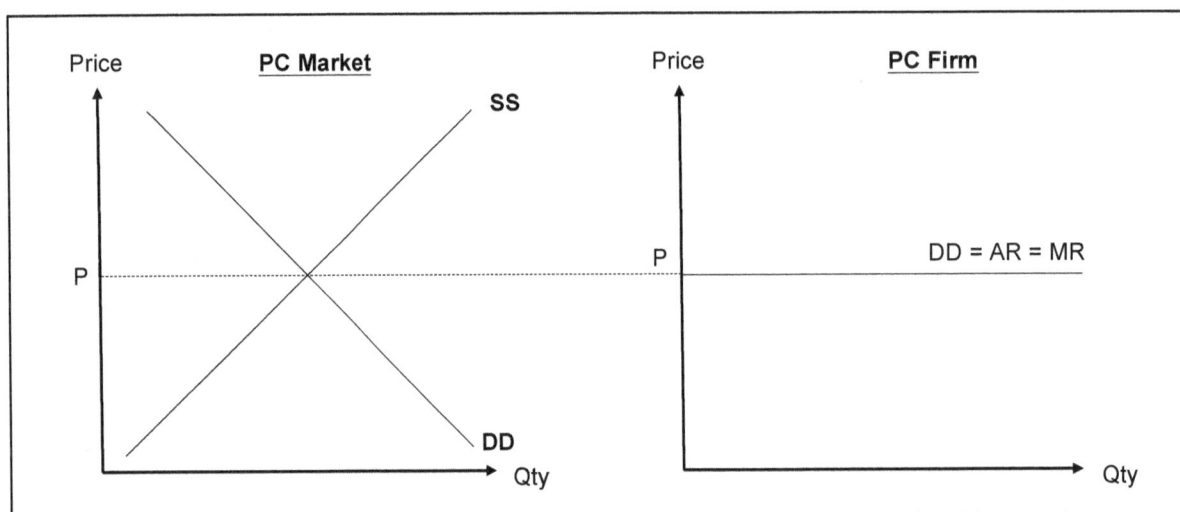

MPC firm

A monopolistically competitive (MPC) firm operates in an **imperfectly competitive** market, in which firms sell products which may be **differentiated** from other firms' products in terms of product quality, advertising, and so on. Consumers who have **different tastes** can exhibit preferences for different firms' products. As rivals' products are not perfect substitutes for firms' products, MPC firms are **price-setters** which have some degree of control over their price. This translates into a **downward sloping demand curve**.

The demand curve for an MPC curve is downward sloping because when the firm raises its price, fewer consumers will be willing and able to purchase the product from this firm and may choose to purchase substitutes from rivals instead, leading to a fall in quantity demanded for the firm's products. However, since rivals' products are **not perfect substitutes**, a number of consumers will still be willing to pay more to purchase this particular firm's products. If the firm were to reduce the price of its good, it would be able to sell more of its good as a greater number of consumers would be willing and able to purchase this product. Thus, unlike the PC firm, the MPC firm is **able to decide what price it wants to charge for the goods it sells.**

Tip

Do not confuse an individual PC firm's demand with the market demand. The market comprises of all the buyers and sellers, and the **market demand curve is still the usual downward-sloping demand curve**. The firm's demand curve is determined by the interaction of the market demand and supply which gives rise to the market price as shown in the previous page.

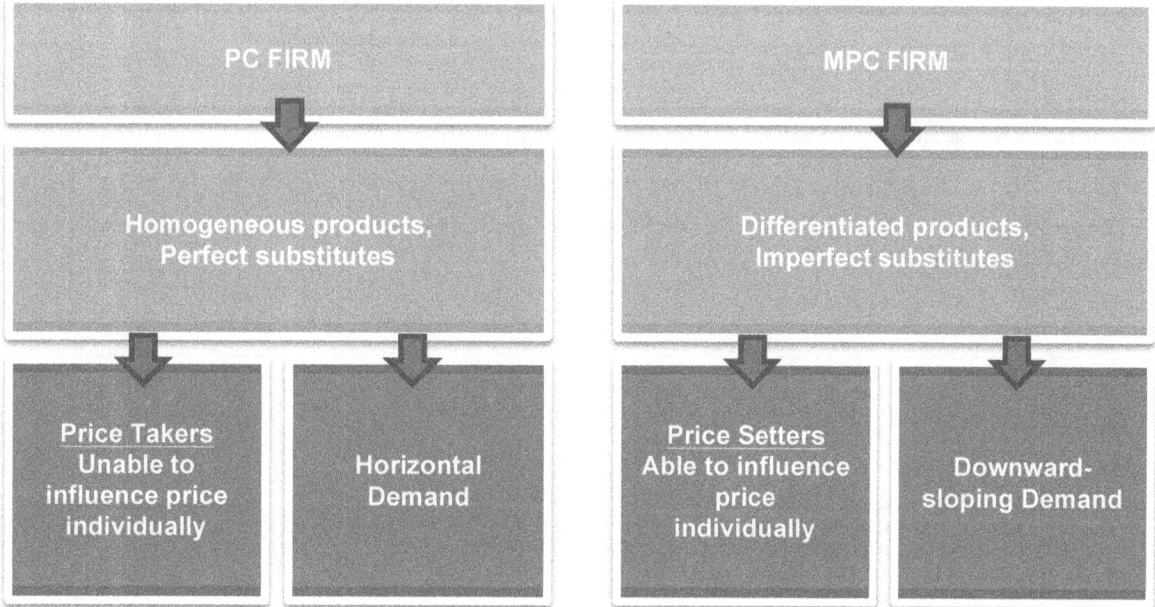

PC FIRM	MPC FIRM
Homogeneous products, Perfect substitutes	Differentiated products, Imperfect substitutes
Price Takers Unable to influence price individually / Horizontal Demand	**Price Setters** Able to influence price individually / Downward-sloping Demand

11. Explain why the Marginal Revenue is below the Average Revenue for firms in imperfect markets.

Average Revenue (AR) is the revenue per unit of output. **Marginal Revenue (MR)** is the additional revenue earned from selling an additional unit of output.

In perfect markets, the AR curve is horizontal and firms have no control over their price-output combination. In imperfect markets however, the AR curve is **downward-sloping**. This means that **firms can decide on how much to sell, and at what price.** However, in order to sell more units of a good, it must lower its price.

In the example below, assuming the firm charges a uniform price for every unit of its product (and does not practice price discrimination), the firm will have to accept a lower price on **all** of its other units in order to sell an extra unit. Thus, **the MR is equal to the price the firm receives from the sale of the last additional unit, minus the loss of revenue from the sale of other units at a lower price.** This is lower than the AR, which is reflected by the prices at every output level. Hence, MR decreases at a faster rate than AR/DD as output level increases.

Price = AR = DD/$	Quantity sold	Total Revenue (TR)/$	Marginal Revenue/$
10	1	10	**10**
9	2	18	18-10 = **8**
8	3	24	24-18 = **6**
7	4	28	28-24 = **4**
6	5	30	30-28 = **2**
5	6	30	30-30 = **0**

This is why MR is always less than AR in an imperfect market structure, for every corresponding output level, except for the first unit. The gradient of the MR curve is also twice that of the AR curve.

12. Explain how PED can be used for pricing strategy.

The PED of a particular product can help suppliers to formulate pricing strategies to increase his or her total revenue.

PED<1
If demand for a firm's product is **price-inelastic** (PED<1), the firm should **raise the price** of their good to increase total revenue. An increase in price would lead to a less than proportionate fall in quantity demanded relative to the increase in price. Since total revenue is Price x Qty (PxQ), this would lead to an increase in the firm's total revenue, ceteris paribus.

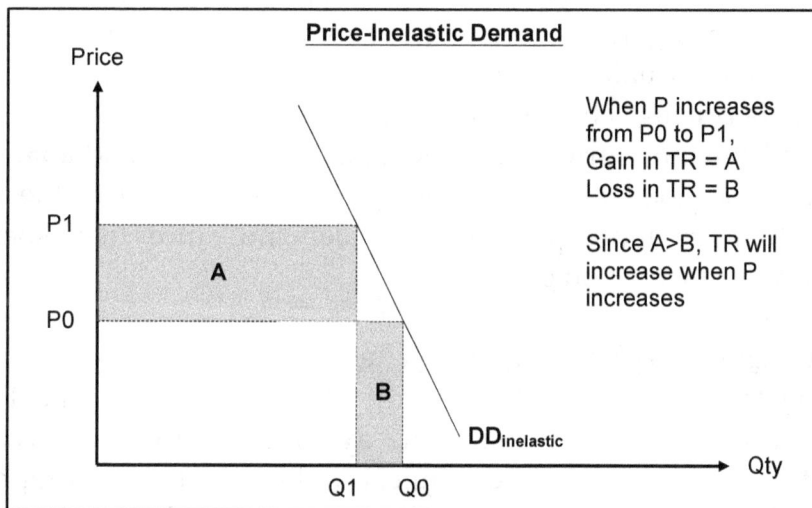

PED>1
If demand for a firm's product is **price-elastic** (PED>1), firms should **lower the price** of their good in order to increase total revenue. A fall in price would lead to a more than proportionate increase in quantity demanded relative to the decrease in price. Thus, ceteris paribus, this would lead to an increase in total revenue (PxQ).

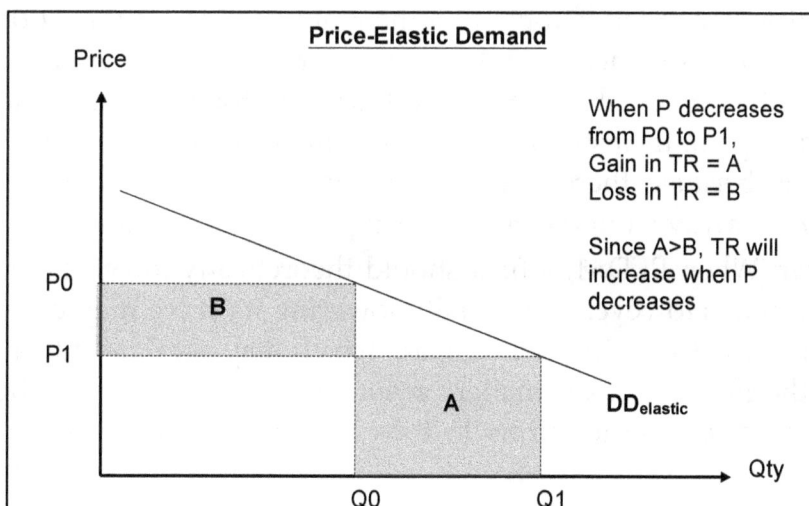

Evaluation:

Price Discrimination
In general, price-setting firms which possess significant market power often experience relatively **price-inelastic demand** for their products, which puts them in a better position to practice **price discrimination**. This is because fewer substitutes are available, reducing the probability of consumers purchasing substitutes instead of paying higher prices for the same good.

In addition, the difference in PED among consumer segments is also the basis for price-discrimination. Assuming the conditions for successful PD are met, firms **can maximize total revenue** (TR) by charging higher prices for submarkets whose PED<1, while charging lower prices for submarkets whose PED>1. While such pricing strategies are usually used to increase TR, it could also be a means to support a **more equitable** pricing scheme, such as charging lower prices to the lower-income (which tend to have more price-elastic demand since they spend **a larger proportion of their income** on goods), while higher prices are charged to the higher-income (which tend to have more price-inelastic demand since they spend a **smaller proportion of their income** on goods).

Technical difficulties in computing PED values
Economic agents often face technical difficulties in gauging the PED values of various products. This may be due to the **dynamic nature** of the economy (which causes data to become outdated very quickly), the difficulty and high costs in **data collection**, or due to **elasticity values differing amongst different consumer groups** (e.g. high income versus low income consumers). An incorrectly computed PED value may cause economic agents to make inappropriate decisions.

Other limitations
- **Ceteris paribus assumption does not hold:** Using PED values is dependent on the assumption that no other variables will change. However, observed changes in quantity demanded/supplied in the real world usually include the effects of multiple factors interacting with one another. Suppose a firm increases the price of its product given the knowledge that PED for the good is less than 1, i.e. demand is price-inelastic. However, the increase in price may turn out to be disastrous because there may at the same time be **a switch in tastes and preferences away from the good**, causing a decrease in demand.
- **Price war:** When PED>1, a firm should theoretically lower its price to increase total revenue. However, continually lowering its price may compel rival firms to do the same to retain market share, which may **escalate into a price war** that causes the firm to make smaller or even subnormal profits. Thus, it may not always be **desirable** for firms to lower their prices even if demand is price-elastic.

13. Explain how technology can affect the market for agriculture.

Demand-side effects

Improvements in technology have brought about the emergence of **biofuels**, which are energy sources derived from living materials (such as agricultural produce). For example, bioethanol is now derived by the fermentation of carbohydrates stored in agricultural produce such as corn and sugarcane. It can then be converted into gasoline additives or used as a fuel for vehicles in its pure form. This results in **increased demand for agriculture** as it now has an alternative usage apart from consumption. This leads to an increase in revenue from $0Q_0E_0P_0$ to $0Q_1E_1P_1$, as illustrated in the following diagram.

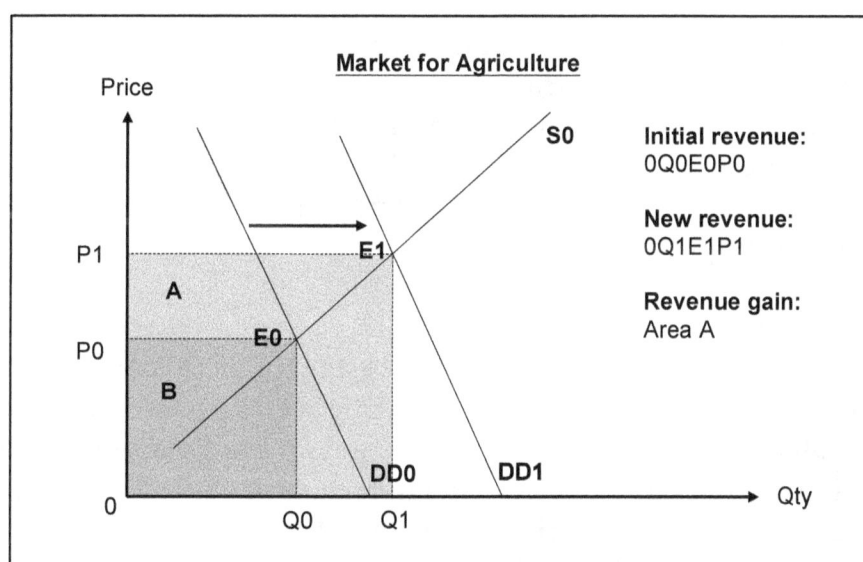

Supply-side effects

Technological advances can increase the supply of agriculture by **lowering the cost of production (COP)** of agricultural produce and **increasing the productivity** of factors of production. For example, the invention of more efficient machines to sow seeds or harvest crops, as well as GM crops which allow for higher yields can help to lower the per unit cost of production, allowing the supply of agricultural produce to increase over time.

However, the impact of supply-side shifts on the equilibrium price and output level in the market for agriculture is in turn dependent on the **PED** of agriculture. Since agricultural products are **necessities** with no **substitutes**, the demand for agricultural products is price-inelastic **(PED<1)**. An increase in the supply of agriculture would therefore lead to **a fall in revenue for farmers** as the fall in revenue from the fall in price is greater than the gain in revenue from the increase in quantity exchanged.

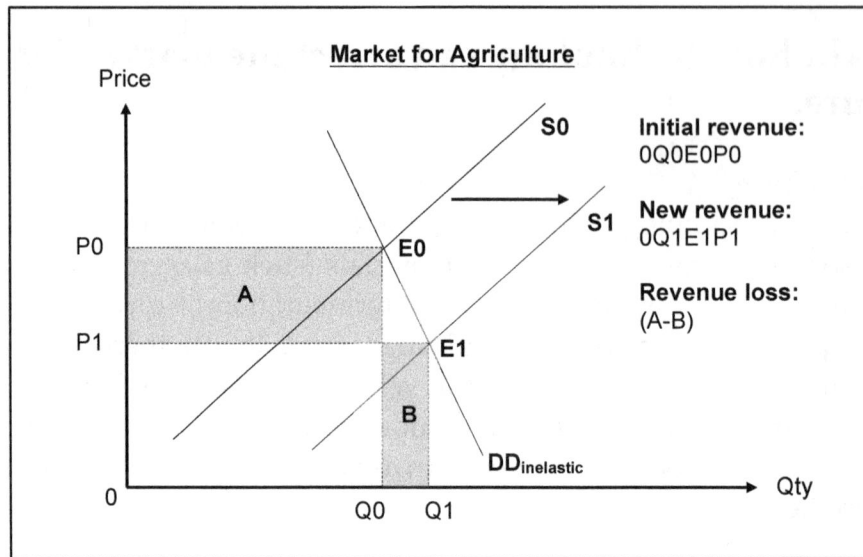

Market for Agriculture

Price

S0

Initial revenue:
0Q0E0P0

S1

New revenue:
0Q1E1P1

Revenue loss:
(A-B)

P0 — E0 — A

P1 — E1 — B

DD$_{inelastic}$

0 — Q0 — Q1 — Qty

As can be seen from the diagram, equilibrium quantity will increase from Q0 to Q1. However, the increase in equilibrium quantity is less than proportionate to the fall in price. The farmers' revenue, which was initially the box 0Q0E0P0, has fallen and the new revenue, represented by the box 0Q1E1P1, is less than the original revenue by the area (A-B). Therefore, ironically, farmers may earn lesser incomes with technological advancements in farming methods.

PES
The supply of agricultural produce tends to be highly price-inelastic (PES<1) due to the long production period (e.g. a minimum time required for crops to be harvested) as well as limited factor mobility (e.g. limited amount of land which can be brought into cultivation). However, advancements in technology would result in the **supply of agriculture becoming more price-elastic** over time. For example, some GM crops can be harvested within a shorter period of time, resulting in a **shorter production period**. In addition, with better storage functions and preservation methods, it may now be more **feasible** to keep stocks of agricultural produce. The use of new technologies such as hydroponics can help to overcome land constraints and also improve **factor mobility**. As such, supply of agricultural produce will become more price-elastic. This can help to reduce price volatility and the instability in farmers' incomes.

Evaluation:

Natural factors (Supply-side effects)
In agriculture, the most significant supply-side factor would be natural factors such as **climatic conditions.** For example, abundant rainfall, the absence of pests and favourable temperatures are all natural factors, which would help to increase the supply of agriculture. As a result, even if technology were to increase supply, if adverse supply shocks occur, the benefits of technological advantages would still be unable to prevent a massive fall in supply as well as a corresponding increase in price and a decrease in quantity exchanged.

22

14. Explain the concepts of scarcity and opportunity cost using the Production Possibility Curve (PPC) model.

The **Production Possibility Curve (PPC)** is a graph that shows the maximum attainable combinations of output which can be produced in an economy **within a specific period of time**, when **all** available resources are **fully and efficiently employed**, and at **a given state of technology**.

In this example, the economy is able to produce two types of goods (capital and consumer goods). Allocating more resources to the production of one type of good, would mean allocating less resources to the production of the other.

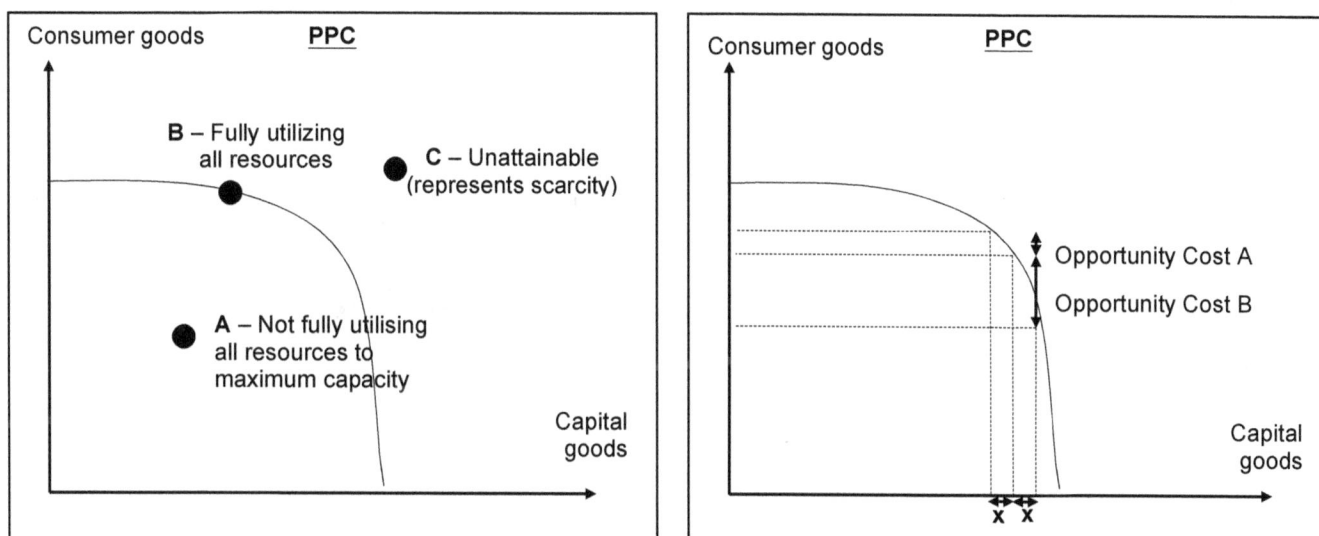

Scarcity is defined as the problem of society having unlimited wants but limited resources. It is represented by the unattainable combinations outside the PPC, given the current amount of resources and the state of technology possessed by the economy. Due to the problem of scarcity, society has to make a **choice** between combinations of the 2 goods (capital/consumer) as resources are limited and cannot fulfill all wants.

Opportunity cost is defined as the cost in terms of the value of the **next best alternative** forgone when an economic decision is made. It arises because of scarcity and is reflected by the downward (negative) slope of the PPC. Since limited resources are already being fully employed to their maximum capacity, to choose to have more of one good would mean having to give up some of the other good. For example, as shown in the diagram, when society decides to produce the first **x** more units of capital goods, it incurs Opportunity Cost A, which is the amount of consumer goods that have to be forgone.

As factors are not perfectly homogeneous or equally suited for the production of all types of goods, as more of a particular good is produced, larger quantities of an alternative good must be sacrificed. As the economy produces a good, it will first deploy resources that are most suitable for the production of the good. However, in order to produce more of the same good, it has to start using resources, which are less and less suitable for its production – resources which might have been better utilized producing other goods. For example, an accountant will not be as skilled at waiting tables as a waiter, and vice versa.

As shown in the diagram, Opportunity Cost A is incurred when the first x units of capital goods are produced instead of consumer goods, but when x *more* units of capital goods are produced, Opportunity Cost B (which is greater than Opportunity Cost A) is incurred. This illustrates the problem of **increasing opportunity cost of production**, and is shown by the PPC curve being **concave** to the origin.

15. Explain how Price Elasticity of Demand (PED) can determine how Consumer Expenditure changes

PED can help to determine how consumer expenditure (CE) changes when there is a change in supply, ceteris paribus. CE is calculated by taking the **Price** paid **multiplied by the quantity consumed. Demand must remain constant** in order to evaluate these changes.

PED<1

For example, since grain is an important food staple in many parts of the world, the DD for grain can be assumed to be price-inelastic, i.e. **PED<1**. An increase in the marginal cost of production of grain will cause the supply curve in the grain market to shift to the left, ceteris paribus, as selling grain becomes less profitable at every price level.

When supply falls from S0 to S1, the shortage at the initial equilibrium price P0, exerts an upward pressure on price, causing quantity supplied to increase and quantity demanded to fall until the new equilibrium is achieved at P1 and Q1. The increase in price leads to a **less than proportionate fall in quantity demanded relative to the price increase**. Thus, **consumer expenditure on grain will increase.**

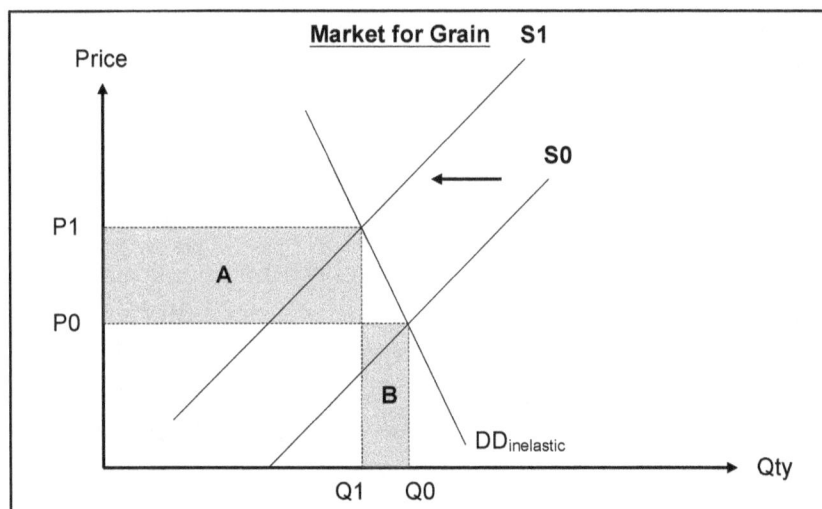

When P increases from P0 to P1,
Increase in consumer expenditure = A (due to increase in P)
Fall in consumer expenditure = B (due to fall in Qty)

Since A>B, consumer expenditure increases when P increases

PED>1

Luxury items such as sports cars take up a large proportion of ordinary citizens' income and are not essential. Therefore, demand for such items can be said to be price-elastic in nature, i.e. **PED>1**. An increase in the marginal cost of production of sports cars will cause the supply curve to shift to the left, ceteris paribus, since selling sports cars becomes less profitable at every price level.

When supply falls from S0 to S1, the shortage at the initial equilibrium price P0, exerts an upward pressure on price, causing quantity supplied to increase and quantity demanded to fall until the new equilibrium, P1 and Q1 is achieved. The

25

increase in price leads to a **more than proportionate fall in quantity demanded relative to the price increase**. Thus, **consumer expenditure on luxury cars will decrease.**

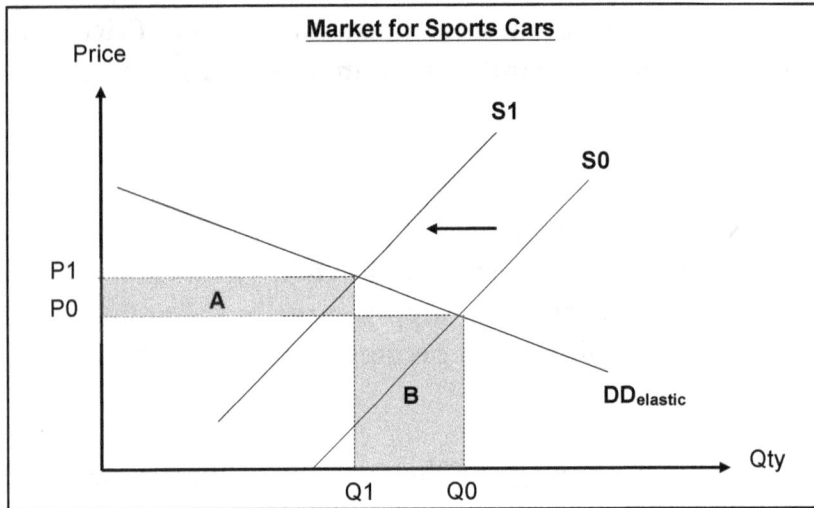

Market for Sports Cars

When P increases from P0 to P1,
Increase in consumer expenditure = A (due to increase in P)
Fall in consumer expenditure = B (due to fall in Qty)

Since A<B, consumer expenditure decreases when P increases

The reverse is true for an increase in supply. When supply increases, the **price of the product will fall**, ceteris paribus. When **PED<1**, the quantity demanded of the product will increase less than proportionately to the decrease in price, leading to a **decrease** in consumer expenditure. When **PED>1**, the quantity demanded of the product will increase more than proportionately to the decrease in price, leading to an **increase** in consumer expenditure.

Evaluation:

However, for the sports car market, it is also very likely that consumers in this market already belong to the high-income segment of the population. Thus, the expenditure may constitute a relatively low proportion of their income, and the overall demand for sports cars may be price-inelastic. As such, when price increases, quantity demanded may actually decrease less than proportionately, and consumer expenditure may actually increase.

16. Explain why oil prices are volatile.

Oil prices are volatile primarily due to **unstable demand and supply conditions**, coupled with a **price-inelastic supply and demand.** This means that changes in demand and supply **both** lead to a **more than proportionate change in price with respect to change in quantity.**

Unstable demand conditions
- Demand for oil is highly **income-elastic.** The demand for oil is therefore highly dependent on changes in income. For example, if incomes increase, demand for private transport (such as cars instead of buses), will tend to increase more than proportionately to the increase in incomes, since private transport is usually regarded as a luxury good. Since there is joint demand for fuel and cars, there will also be a more than proportionate increase in the demand for oil relative to the increase in income.
- Thus, demand for oil tends to be **cyclical**, which means that it fluctuates according to patterns of economic growth: Demand for oil tends to increase significantly during economic booms, and decrease significantly during recessions.
- In addition, a major source of the demand for oil is **speculative.** This means that people choose to buy or sell oil depending on their expectations of future oil prices. For example, if the price of oil is expected to rise, then the demand for oil will now increase, perhaps to stock up more oil now which can be resold later at higher prices. As expectations change according to the state of the economy, the political climate, supply conditions and so on, demand for oil can undergo significant fluctuations within a short period of time, leading to volatile prices.

Price-inelastic supply
- The supply of oil tends to be **price-inelastic** in the short term. This is because the quantity supplied of oil cannot be readily adjusted when changes in price occur, since a finite number of oil wells exist and the process of extracting and refining oil is often highly complex. In addition, time is usually required to build the necessary infrastructure to begin production.
- As such, when demand changes occur, they will lead to a **more than proportionate change in price with respect to changes in quantity**, as shown in the following diagram, where price increases sharply from P0 to P1. This further increases the volatility of oil prices. Contrast this against the case of PES>1, also shown in the following diagram, in which price only increases from P0 to P2.

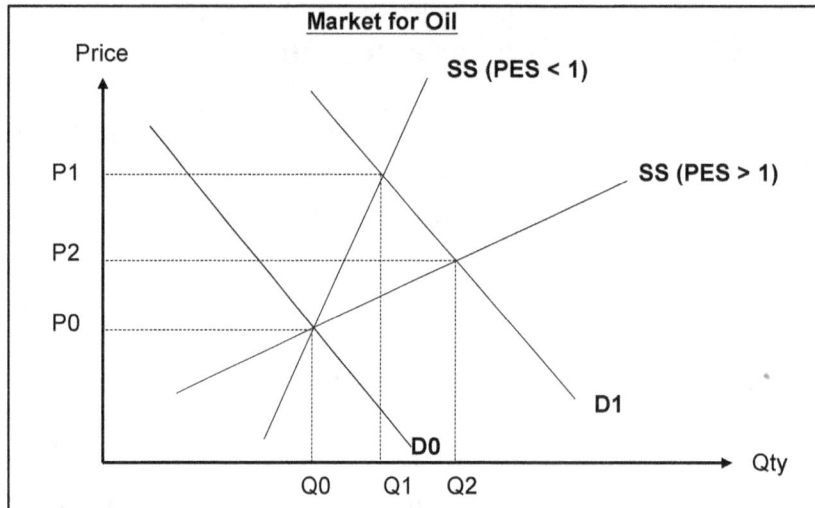

Market for Oil

Price

SS (PES < 1)

SS (PES > 1)

P1
P2
P0

D1

D0

Q0   Q1   Q2

Qty

Unstable Supply Conditions

- In addition, the oil market faces unstable supply conditions. This is because the supply of oil is dependent on the discovery of new oil wells and the rate at which oil reserves are depleted. Furthermore, the supply of oil is often subjected to political conditions. For example, political conflicts and crises are fairly common in the Middle East, where most of the world's oil reserves are located and supply disruptions could occur such as due to Libya's quite recent civil war.

Price-inelastic demand

- The demand for oil also tends to be **price-inelastic** in the short term. This is because there is hardly any close substitute available for its use (as a source of energy) in production and it is complementary to the habitual consumption patterns (such as driving and cooking) of individuals.
- As such, when supply changes occur, they will lead to a **more than proportionate change in price with respect to change in quantity**, as shown in the diagram below, where price decreases from P0 to P1, as a result of an increase in supply. Contrast this against the case of PED>1, also shown in the diagram below, in which price only decreases from P0 to P2.

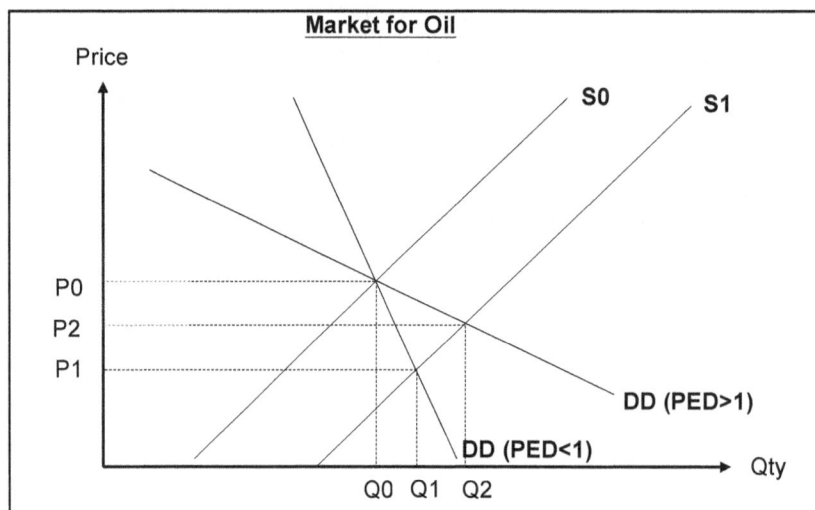

Market for Oil

Price

S0   S1

P0
P2
P1

DD (PED>1)

DD (PED<1)

Q0 Q1 Q2

Qty

Evaluation:

<u>Organisation of Petroleum Exporting Countries (OPEC)</u>
The OPEC controls about 40% of the world's supply of oil. It is an example of a **cartel**, which is a form of **collusive behaviour** in oligopolies where firms formally collude to fix prices, for example, by restricting industry output to set high prices. Each individual firm is given a production quota, and collectively act as a monopoly to maximize joint profits. However, although **in theory OPEC has the ability to intervene through output quotas to fix oil prices**, this may be difficult in practice due to unstable demand conditions, different objectives amongst the different member countries, as well as actions taken by other oil producers.

> **Tip**
>
> Never say that a good is price- or income- elastic/inelastic. It is the **demand** for the good which is price or income- elastic/inelastic, not the good itself. .

17. Explain the difference between scarcity and shortage.

Resources used to produce goods and services are finite, yet consumers' wants are unlimited. This is the universal problem of **scarcity**. Thus, economic agents are forced to make choices to allocate their scarce resources between alternative uses to achieve the greatest utility (satisfaction) or maximise their welfare. Thus, the problem of **opportunity cost** arises. Opportunity cost is defined as the cost in terms of the value of the next best alternative, which has to be forgone.

A shortage, on the other hand, occurs when **quantity demanded exceeds quantity supplied** at a given price. This occurs when the price is lower than the free market equilibrium price, and may be a result of an increase in demand for a good or a fall in the supply of a good, ceteris paribus.

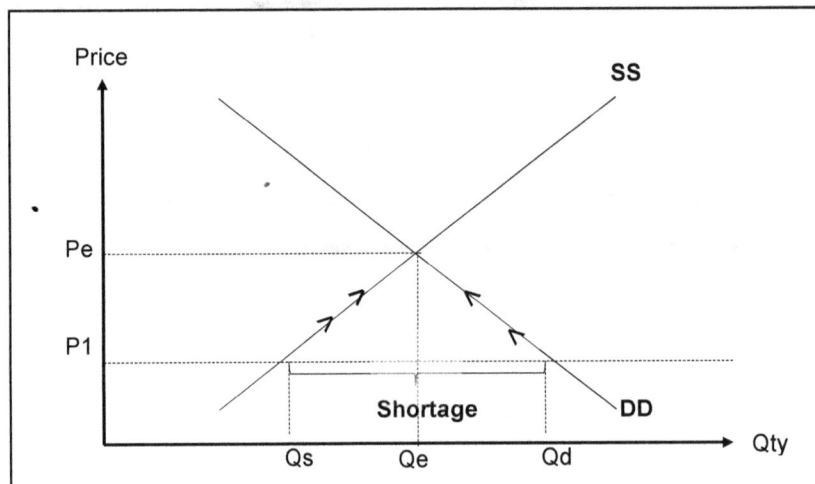

Referring to the diagram above, when a shortage occurs, the price mechanism will act to correct the shortage. As the shortage **exerts an upward pressure on price**, quantity demanded of the good will fall since fewer consumers are now willing and able to consume the good. At the same time, quantity supplied increases as more producers are willing and able to sell additional units of the good, since profitability has increased. Thus, the new equilibrium output (Qe) and price (Pe) are achieved, where Pe will be higher than the original price (P1), and the shortage is eliminated as Quantity demanded = Quantity supplied at Qe.

There will always be scarcity since there will always be limited resources and unlimited wants. However, shortages can be eliminated **with an increase in price** to a new, higher equilibrium price.

18. Explain Income Elasticity of Demand and give examples of its applications.

The **Income Elasticity of Demand (YED)** is a measure of the responsiveness of the demand of a good to changes in the consumer's income, ceteris paribus. It measures how much **the entire demand curve** (*and not quantity demanded*) will shift in response to a change in consumers' income levels.

$$\text{Formula: YED} = \frac{\%\ change\ in\ quantity\ demanded}{\%\ change\ in\ income} = \frac{\Delta Q}{\Delta Y} \times \frac{Y0}{Q0}$$

Sign of Coefficient	Coefficient	Interpretation
Negative (YED < 0) **Inferior good**	YED < 0	Increase in Y will lead to a *decrease* in demand for the good, because inferior goods can be replaced by other more desirable goods as income increases. E.g. Cheap staple foodstuffs such as broken rice
Positive (YED > 0) **Normal good**	0 < YED < 1	Demand for good is **income-inelastic.** Good is a **necessity.** Percentage increase in Y produces a *smaller percentage increase* in DD. E.g. Food, clothing, housing
	YED > 1	Demand for good is **income-elastic.** Good is a **luxury good**. Percentage increase in Y produces a *larger percentage increase* in DD. E.g. Branded watches, handbags, cars, etc.

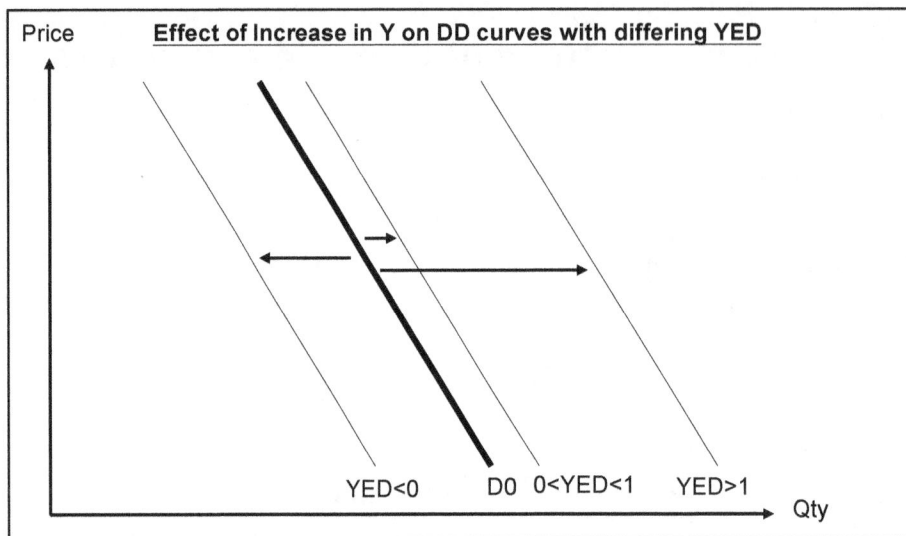

Price — Effect of Increase in Y on DD curves with differing YED

YED<0   D0   0<YED<1   YED>1   Qty

Knowledge of YED can be useful for output planning and marketing strategies. For example, it can help producers to respond to changes in income, and to segment their market into different income groups in order to maximize their profits.

YED Applications

Responding to Income Changes

When incomes are expected to rise, firms should reduce output or shift out of the production of inferior goods (if any) and increase their output of normal goods, especially luxury goods. They may also rebrand their existing products as more prestigious or create more premium versions of existing products in order to experience a greater increase in demand for their good when income increases.

Conversely, **when incomes are expected to fall,** firms should direct resources away from the production of luxury goods and shift into the production of inferior goods, or produce goods which have a more income-inelastic demand (such as necessities). They could also focus their marketing efforts on those who perceive the good to be essential, or create more basic versions of their existing luxury products.

Segmenting markets

Firms can segment their markets into different income groups and sell different ranges of products to suit consumers of different income groups. Knowledge of the YED values will help producers to classify their goods according to whether they are necessities or luxuries. As a result, firms will sell more necessities in mass-market locations, whilst selling more luxuries in high-income districts.

For example, a supermarket which has outlets located in an upper-class income district can carry items which have higher positive income elasticity of demand, such as organic foods, while outlets located in the heartlands may carry more goods with lower income elasticity of demand such as basic food necessities.

Evaluation:

<u>YED Limitations</u>

- Usually, the more basic an item is in a household's consumption pattern, the lower its income elasticity of demand. However, this differs from household to household, depending on its income level. Hence, it may be difficult to compute the YED value of a certain good since this tends to differ from household to household. This is also why the YED values of a good tend to differ when comparing between a developed and developing country.

- It may be **difficult to predict income changes** due to the dynamic and unpredictable nature of the economy. Firms usually need time to plan for whether to produce more basic or more premium versions of their good. They may also require more time to redesign and repackage their goods. This means that application of YED may require forecasting income changes, which could turn out to be incorrect.

Tip

Most primary sector products are characterized by a low YED. Demand for secondary sector products (such as manufactured products) are more income-elastic while demand for tertiary sector products (service industry) are even more income-elastic in nature. Therefore as incomes in an economy grow, we can expect the following structural transformation in an economy: The relative size of the primary sector will shrink while the relative size of the tertiary sector will typically rise.

APPLICATIONS OF YED

Responding to Y Changes

Y increase
- Reduce output of inferior goods, increase output of normal (especially luxury) goods
- Create more premium versions of existing products
- Brand existing products as more luxurious

Y decrease
- Reduce output of luxury goods, increase output of necessities and inferior goods
- Create more basic versions of existing products
- Brand existing products as value-for-money

Segmenting Markets

- Classify goods according to whether they are necessities or luxuries based on YED values
- Sell more luxuries in higher-income districts, and more necessities in mass-market districts/heartlands

19. Explain Cross Elasticity of Demand and give examples of its applications

The **Cross Elasticity of Demand (CED)** is a measure of the responsiveness of demand for a good to a change in price of another good, ceteris paribus. It measures how much **demand** will change in response to a given change in price of another good, ceteris paribus. This is represented by a shift of the entire demand curve.

Sign of coefficient	Coefficient	Interpretation
Negative (CED < 0) The two goods are **complements.** Increase in price of one good will lead to a fall in demand of the other good.	CED < 0	The larger the absolute value of the negative CED, the greater the complementarity between the two goods and the more responsive demand will be to changes in the price of the other good.
N/A (CED = 0) The two goods are **unrelated.**	CED = 0	Change in price of one good does not affect demand for the other.
Positive (CED > 0) Goods are **substitutes.** Increase in price of one good will lead to increase in demand of the other good.	0 < CED < 1	The two goods are not very close substitutes. Increase in the price of one good will lead to a less than proportionate increase in demand of the other good.
	CED > 1	The two goods are close substitutes. Increase in the price of one good will lead to a more than proportionate increase in demand of the other good

CED Applications

Knowledge of CED can help firms plan their pricing policies as well as their marketing strategies.

Pricing policies
When the price of a **substitute** good falls, using the knowledge of CED, firms will know that a fall in demand for their good can be expected and therefore to maintain sales, they may have to respond by matching the price cut. This is especially so when rivals' goods are **close substitutes.**

Price cuts can be achieved by striving to be as cost-efficient as possible in the firms' operations so as to lower costs and thus be able to match their rival's price. In some instances, firms may even be able to "squeeze" out competition by selling their good at an even lower price. If the firm is not willing to lower its price, then it should be prepared to decrease output given the decrease in demand.

<u>Marketing and sales strategies</u>

CED values can help firms to ascertain who is/are their closest rivals, and focus on monitoring them and responding to their actions. A firm will also strive to make its goods less substitutable by its rival's goods so that it will be less affected by pricing policies of rival firms. This can be achieved through **product differentiation**, which involves creating **real or imaginary differences** to its product, thus helping to cultivate brand loyalty. **Real differences** include adding novel features to their product, improving its workmanship and design, or the quality of materials used; **imaginary differences** involve the use of advertising and marketing strategies to inform, persuade and convince consumers that the product is unique. Firms can also attempt to improve the **conditions of sale** such as by the ambience and location of retail outlets and the quality of the service offered.

An example of product differentiation would be Starbucks Coffee, which has branded itself as a leader in coffee production by using coffee beans of the highest quality and utilising state-of-the-art technological processes to enhance its coffee brewing processes. It has also sought to differentiate its conditions of sale by improving the atmosphere of its coffeehouses and the service of its staff.

Firms will try to leverage on **complementary goods** to increase sales by linking their marketing plans to that of the other firm. They can collaborate or build alliances with firms selling complementary goods, and engage in joint promotions, which will promote the sale of both goods. The Star Alliance is an example of an alliance between airlines, which seek to complement each others' operations by sharing their route structures and customer loyalty programmes, enabling each airline to benefit from greater demand and revenue.

Alternately, firms can package complementary goods together: For example, tour agencies and airline companies can create travel packages encompassing both airline and tour services. By offering an attractive package price, demand and revenue for both the airlines and tour agencies can increase.

Evaluation

<u>CED Limitations</u>

- CED values are premised on the **ceteris paribus** assumption. However, in reality, many other supply and demand factors may be changing simultaneously. For example, in markets where rivals closely watch and react to firms' strategies, a decrease in a rival firm's price could prompt a firm to match the price cut. However, this may be a disadvantageous move as the rival firm's price cut may be the result of a change in consumers' tastes and preferences which has led to a fall in demand for its product. This actually benefits the firm as the change of tastes and preferences is in their favour and will lead to an increase in demand for its good, which justifies a higher price instead.

- Data on other firms' strategies may be limited as it would be in their own interests to veil their actions, making it difficult for rival firms to respond. For example, petrol stations have a published price but actually provide various other discounts and rebates.

- It may not be feasible to continually match rivals' price cuts in oligopolistic markets as this may eventually lead to a **price war** that results in lower revenue and profits for all.

- **Joint promotions** may be costly and it may be difficult to negotiate deals which are mutually beneficial for both parties. For example, a movie ticket and popcorn combo must be able to increase profits for both the cinema as well as the popcorn maker company, or either party may choose not to engage in the promotion.

- CED data may become inaccurate and irrelevant to firms due to dynamic changes in the economy, and must be computed regularly to be used effectively.

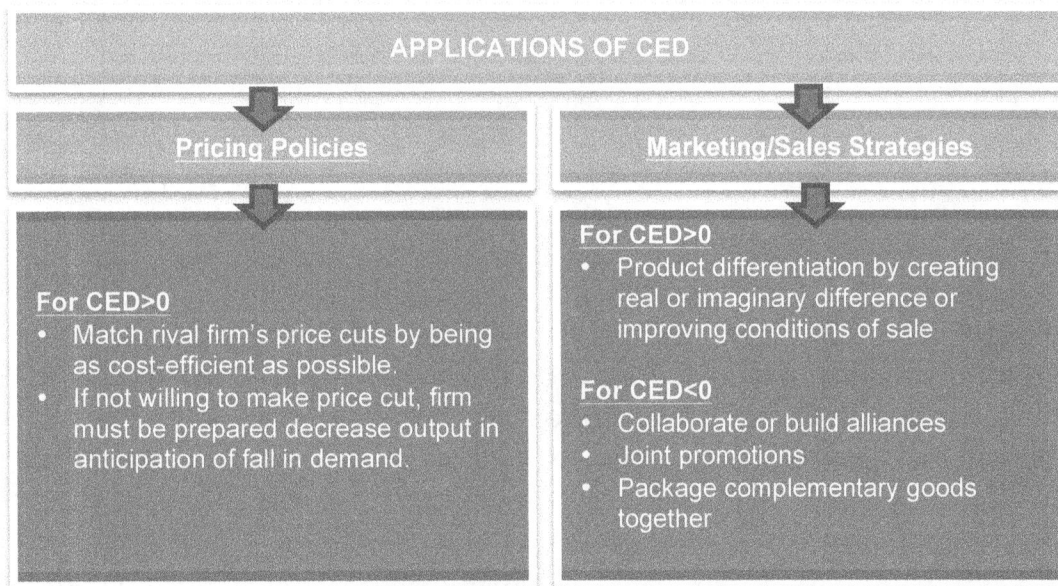

APPLICATIONS OF CED	
Pricing Policies	**Marketing/Sales Strategies**
For CED>0 • Match rival firm's price cuts by being as cost-efficient as possible. • If not willing to make price cut, firm must be prepared decrease output in anticipation of fall in demand.	For CED>0 • Product differentiation by creating real or imaginary difference or improving conditions of sale For CED<0 • Collaborate or build alliances • Joint promotions • Package complementary goods together

20. Explain the effects of a Price Ceiling

A price ceiling is a **legally-established maximum price to prevent prices from rising above a certain level**. It prohibits producers from selling above the stipulated price, and is usually put in place for **equity** reasons: To make goods and services, especially necessities like food and housing, affordable to lower-income earners.

In order to be effective, a price ceiling must be set **below** the market equilibrium price.

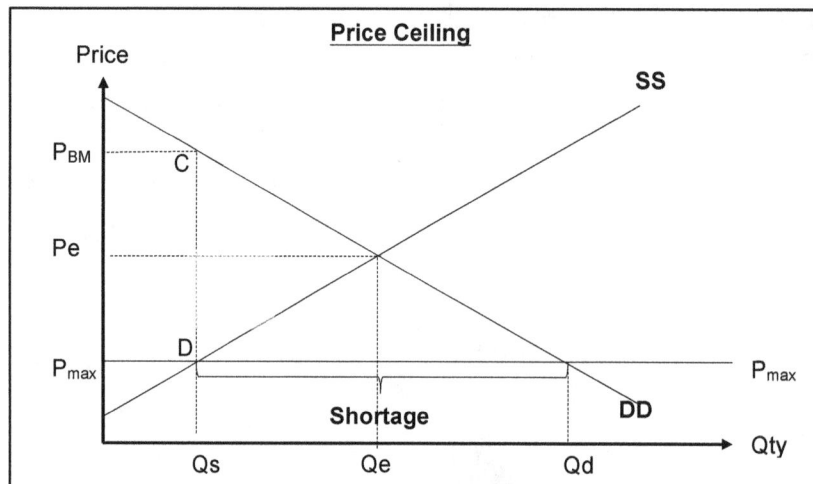

Effects of a Price Ceiling

Shortage
At Pmax, **quantity demanded exceeds quantity supplied**, leading to a **shortage** equivalent to (Qd-Qs). However, prices are no longer able to rise and serve as a rationing tool to eliminate the shortage.

Non-price rationing
As a result, producers may resort to other means to ration their goods amongst consumers. Since producers can decide whom they wish to sell their goods to, this may lead to seller preference and discrimination. For example, producers may only sell the good to favoured customers, or rationing coupons may have to be issued amongst those who wish to purchase the good. In other instances, a non-discriminatory 'first come first serve' policy may be administered to ration the good. Nevertheless, the **original intended beneficiaries of the policy may end up losing out**, as now they may not be able to obtain the good at all.

Black markets
Since there is a shortage, some people will be willing to pay a price above the price ceiling to get hold of the good. Thus, a black market may result with black

marketeers selling goods illegally **above the maximum price**, enabling them to profiteer. In the most extreme scenario where black marketeers are able to obtain all the goods, Pb represents the maximum black market price that consumers will be willing and able to pay the black market for the good. In this instance, the black marketeer is able to earn profit represented by $PmaxP_{BM}CD$.

Worsening Equity

If the good is sold in the black market, the price of the good may now be even higher than the previous free market equilibrium Pe and now the lower-income will not be able to obtain the good if they are unable to pay black market prices. This worsens equity.

Allocative Inefficiency

The free market equilibrium Qe is the socially optimal output (in the absence of externalities and imperfect information), yet only Qs is produced, which means that **too few resources** have been allocated to the production of this good. For all units of the good underproduced, the marginal benefit to society is greater than the marginal cost to society of producing that particular unit. Therefore, societal welfare is not maximised.

Allocative inefficiency results and there is a **deadweight welfare loss** to society, which is equivalent to area (B+C) as shown in the following diagram.

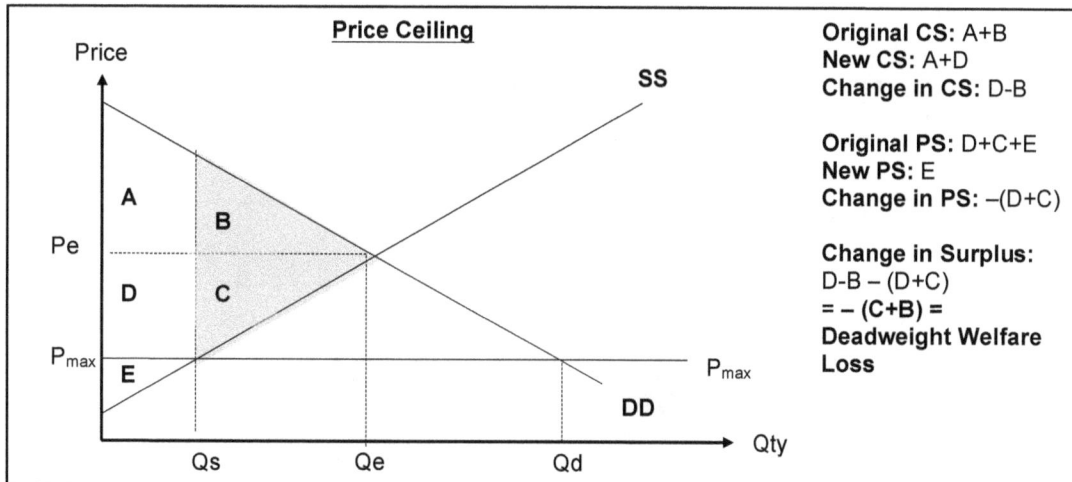

Macro Link:

Price ceilings are also a method to control Inflation, which is a macroeconomic goal. However, history has shown that price ceilings typically do not work and will result in worsening inflation, as consumers will be forced to purchase at black market prices.

Evaluation:

<u>Degree of shortage</u>
The degree of the shortage is dependent on the price elasticity of demand and supply. Over time, if PED and PES values increase (which is usually the case when a longer time period is given), the extent of the shortage will worsen.

<u>Increase in consumer surplus</u>
There is a possibility that consumers may be better off, that is, consumer surplus may increase after the imposition of the price ceiling. Although a price ceiling causes quantity consumed to fall, thus lowering consumer surplus, the fall in price from Pe to Pmax causes consumer surplus to increase. Thus, depending on the relative sizes of areas D and B, consumers may or may not experience an increase in consumer surplus. If area D is greater than area B, consumer surplus will increase.

The more price-elastic the demand for the good, the more likely an increase in consumer surplus will occur. This is because price-sensitive consumers would tend to have more to gain from the fall in price than to lose from the lesser quantity consumed.

21. Explain the rationale for and the effects of an Agricultural Price Support.

An agricultural price support is an example of a **price floor**, which is **a legally established minimum price to prevent prices from falling below a certain level**. Like a price ceiling, it is usually implemented to promote **equity** by ensuring income support for farmers since they are guaranteed a certain level of revenue.

In order to be effective, a price floor must be set **above** the market equilibrium price.

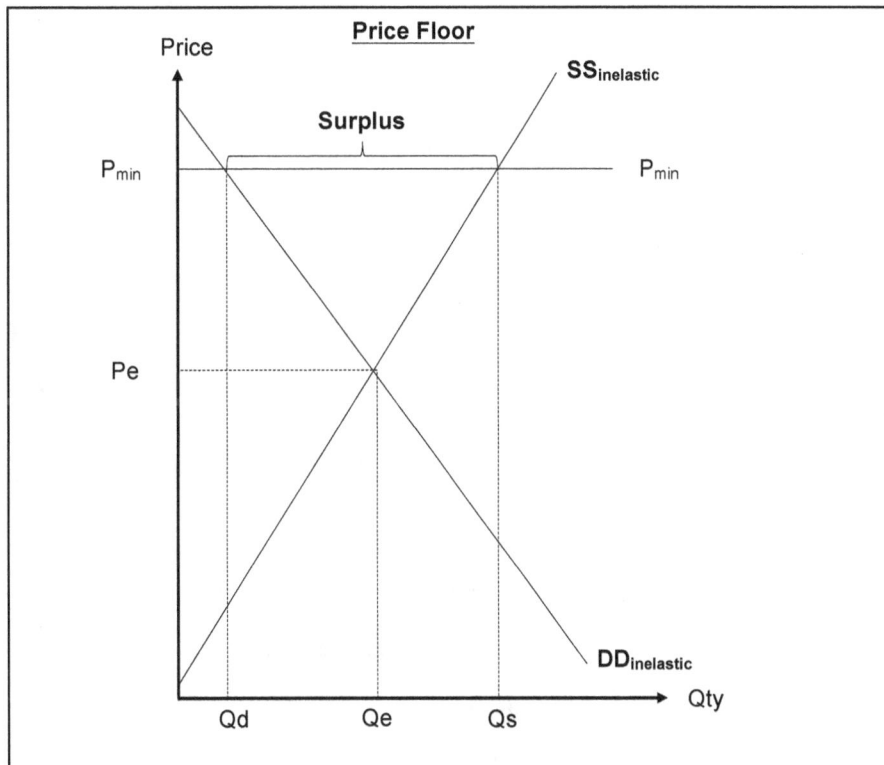

Rationale for an Agricultural Price Support

Agricultural Price Supports are most commonly implemented because of the **volatile and unpredictable nature** of the agricultural industry. Since agricultural foodstuffs are considered necessities and without substitutes, the demand for these goods is price-inelastic. Furthermore, given the lengthy and complex duration of growing agricultural crops, supply of agricultural produce tends to be price-inelastic as well. As such, with PED and PES both < 1, coupled with supply conditions which are highly unpredictable due to weather and climatic conditions, highly volatile prices occur. **As volatile prices will lead to an unstable income for farmers,** agricultural price supports are implemented to stabilise farmers' incomes.

For example, as shown in the following diagram, when supply increases due to favourable climatic conditions or due to a bumper harvest, there will be a less than proportionate increase in quantity demanded (Q1 to Q2) relative to the decrease in price (P1 to P2). Consequently, farmers' revenues and incomes will fall. Thus, in this instance, an agricultural price support will help to stabilise farmers' incomes by eliminating fluctuations due to shocks in the agricultural industry.

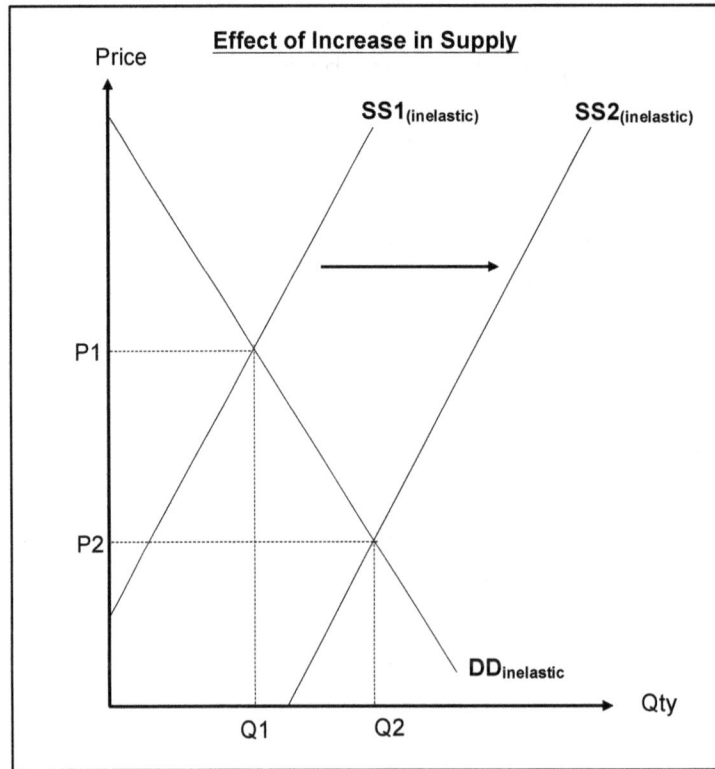

Effect of Increase in Supply

(Diagram: Price on vertical axis, Qty on horizontal axis. Two upward-sloping inelastic supply curves labelled $SS1_{(inelastic)}$ and $SS2_{(inelastic)}$, with an arrow showing a rightward shift from SS1 to SS2. A downward-sloping demand curve labelled $DD_{inelastic}$. SS1 intersects DD at price P1 and quantity Q1; SS2 intersects DD at price P2 and quantity Q2, where P2 < P1 and Q2 > Q1.)

Effects of an Agricultural Price Support

Surplus
At P_{min}, quantity supplied exceeds quantity demanded, thus creating a surplus equivalent to (Qs-Qd) as prices are no longer allowed to fall to eliminate the surplus. Therefore, the agricultural price support scheme is often accompanied by **guaranteed purchase** by the government, which must buy up the surplus to ensure that the agricultural price support serves its purpose of stabilizing farmers' incomes.

Consumer and Producer Surplus
As shown in the following diagram, consumer surplus is reduced, since prices have increased and quantity consumed has fallen. Consumer surplus has in fact been transferred to the producers who benefit from an increase in their surplus.

<u>Allocative Inefficiency</u>

The free market equilibrium Qe is the socially optimal output (in the absence of externalities), yet Qs is produced which means that **too much resources** have been allocated to the production of this good. Furthermore, due to the guaranteed revenue, **new producers may be attracted to enter the market**, creating even greater surpluses. For all the units of the good overproduced, the marginal benefit to society (reflected by the DD curve) is less than the marginal cost to society (reflected by the SS curve) of producing that particular unit.

Thus, this leads to a **deadweight welfare loss** equivalent to the area (C+E+I+H+G) shown in the following diagram.

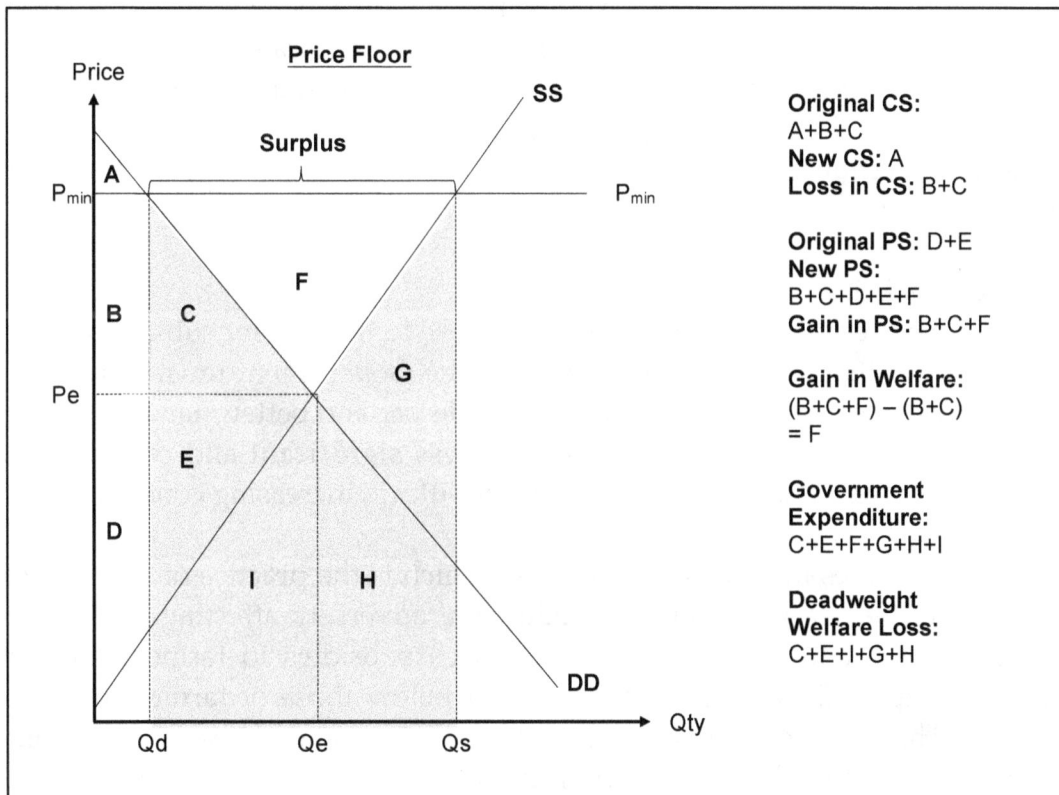

Price Floor

Original CS:
A+B+C
New CS: A
Loss in CS: B+C

Original PS: D+E
New PS:
B+C+D+E+F
Gain in PS: B+C+F

Gain in Welfare:
(B+C+F) – (B+C)
= F

Government
Expenditure:
C+E+F+G+H+I

Deadweight
Welfare Loss:
C+E+I+G+H

Evaluation:

<u>Opportunity Cost/Strain on Government Budget</u>

Since the government guarantees purchase of the surplus, **additional costs** will have to be incurred in purchasing, storing, destroying or exporting the surplus. For example, the government will incur storage costs if the additional goods are stockpiled, or will have to provide subsidies to make the good price-competitive in overseas markets. This poses a strain on the government budget and incurs an opportunity cost, as the money could have been better spent on other areas which would have benefited the economy to a greater extent, such as fiscal stimulus or infrastructure development.

Productive Inefficiency
Inefficient firms with higher costs of production no longer have an incentive to cut costs, since their profits are now protected by the minimum price. Firms may also have less incentive to engage in R&D to develop more cost-efficient production methods.

Quality of product
The quality of crops produced may deteriorate as farmers may just produce more units of crops, regardless of their quality, since they are guaranteed a price of P_{min} for their crops.

Worsening Income Inequality
Ironically, it may be the large farming firms which benefit the most from such policies, as they possess the resources to increase their scale of production, increase output, enjoy internal economies of scale and sell a greater amount of output than other farmers, at the minimum price P_{min}. As a result, they will earn an even higher guaranteed revenue than smaller farms which may not be able to increase output by the same extent, thus exacerbating income inequality.

Alternative policies
Instead of a price floor, governments can choose to implement subsidies. The benefit of a subsidy is that there is **no surplus** that the Government must purchase and so the government's expenditure could be much lesser and better managed. In addition, the amount of deadweight loss tends to be **less significant** and consumers will be able to benefit from a lower price and greater output, increasing consumer surplus.

However, subsidies may lead to **dumping**, which is the practice of selling exports at prices below the marginal cost of production, adversely affecting farmers in other countries. For example, European Union (EU) subsidies to farmers have enabled farmers to export their produce at prices far below those of farmers in developing countries. This threatens the livelihood of the latter, and worsens the incomes gap between the developed and developing countries.

Price Floors and Ceilings

In the case of a price ceiling, the amount of the good exchanged is the quantity supplied at that price as it is less than the quantity demanded ($Q_s < Q_d$), while in the case of a price floor, the amount of the good exchanged is the quantity demanded at that price as it is less than the quantity supplied ($Q_d < Q_s$).

This is important to note when trying to determine the effect of price ceilings and floors on consumer and producer surplus. Remember to focus only on the new, lower quantity that will be exchanged.

22. Using 4 examples (Firm, Consumer, Government, Economy), explain the concept of Opportunity Cost.

Opportunity cost is defined as the **cost in terms of the value of the next best alternative that has to be forgone**, or the highest value activity which has to be given up when a particular decision is made. It arises because **wants** are **infinite**, whereas the **resources** available to meet wants are **finite** (due to scarcity) so not all wants can be fulfilled.

Government
For example, if the government decides to invest $100m in building a public school, the opportunity cost incurred by the government could be improved transport infrastructure, a new hospital, and so on. Thus, the government must take into account and consider the benefits of improving the transport infrastructure (which is the opportunity cost) against the benefits of a new public school before making this decision.

Firm
If a farmer decides to grow corn as food, the opportunity cost incurred would be the profits he could have earned if the time, land and other resources were diverted to growing other crops (such as tomatoes, wheat and strawberries) instead. Therefore to really know if the firm is making the best economic decision in producing a certain good, there is a need to differentiate between accounting and economic profits.

Accounting profit refers to a firm's profit, which is calculated by the firm's **total revenue (TR)** minus the firm's **total explicit costs (TC)**, where explicit costs refer to the costs incurred when the firm has to purchase factors of production. On the other hand, economic profit refers to a firm's profit when total opportunity costs have been taken into account, and is calculated by the **firm's total revenue (TR)** minus the firm's **total explicit *and* implicit costs**, where implicit costs refer to the opportunity costs of producing the good as a result of using factors of production that are owned by the firm.

Accounting Profit = TR – Explicit Costs
Economic Profit = TR – (Explicit Costs + Implicit Costs)

For example, an author will need to pay for printing services. These are explicit costs. Implicit costs are a result of the time taken to author a book, which could have been used to teach, thus teaching incomes are forgone.

Economic profits are thus lesser than accounting profits. Most importantly, they will help a firm ascertain if it is making the optimal decision in producing a good (when earning at least zero economic profits) or should shut down and switch to its next best alternative (when earning subnormal profits in the long run).

<u>Consumer</u>

If a student decides to spend $15 on a T-shirt, his opportunity cost would be the satisfaction which could have been obtained by purchasing other items, such as food and drink, textbooks, stationery and so on.

<u>Economy</u>

Assume that an economy can choose to produce 2 types of goods – consumer goods and capital goods. If the economy chooses to produce more consumer goods, the opportunity cost would be the higher **future** standard of living which society could have enjoyed if the economy had chosen to invest in capital goods instead. Conversely, if the economy chooses to produce more capital goods, the opportunity cost would be the higher **current** standard of living which society could have enjoyed if more consumer goods had been produced instead.

Evaluation:

<u>Problems with measuring Opportunity Cost</u>

Calculating opportunity cost requires time and information, which might not always be readily available. Furthermore, it is often difficult to quantify opportunity cost accurately (e.g. quantifying the value of a new public hospital to society).

23. Explain the difference between Fixed costs and Variable costs.

Point of Comparison	Fixed Costs	Variable Costs
Factors of production	Incurred by the use of **fixed factors of production**	Incurred by the use of **variable factors of production**
Examples	Rental costs, costs of heavy machinery	Wage costs of daily rated workers, costs of utilities, raw material costs
Time period	Only fixed in the **short run**; in the long run, all factors are variable except the level of technology	Applicable to both the **short run** and the **long run**
Types	**Total Fixed Costs (TFC)** • **Do not vary with the level of output** • **Must be paid even when there is no production** 	**Total Variable Costs (TVC)** • **Vary directly with output levels – increase as output increases** • **Not incurred when there is no production.**

		• Initially, TVC will rise at a decreasing rate due to the specialization of variable factors of production, and more efficient use of fixed factors. • Eventually, the **law of diminishing marginal returns (LMDR)** sets in. More and more variable factors are applied/added to fixed factors, leading to diminishing marginal returns as each additional variable factor hired now produces less and less additional output. • TVC will begin to rise at an increasing rate as poorer factor combinations set in at higher output levels.
	Average Fixed Costs (AFC) • Defined as Total Fixed Costs **per unit of output (TFC/Q)** • Rectangular hyperbola: Costs decrease continually as output increases as overhead costs are spread over a wider range of output. ![AFC graph: $/Costs on vertical axis, Qty on horizontal axis, AFC curve shown as rectangular hyperbola]	**Average Variable Costs (AVC)** • Defined as Total Variable Costs **per unit of output (TVC/Q)** • U-shaped curve: Costs eventually begin to rise due to LDMR ![AVC graph: $/Costs on vertical axis, Qty on horizontal axis, AVC curve shown as U-shape]

Evaluation:

Greater Internal Economies of Scale
High fixed costs could lead to the possibility of reaping internal economies of scale. Fixed costs tend to be a result of **indivisible factors**, which only exist in minimum sizes and/or large units. For example, large and costly machines can help to speed up processes significantly, but can only be utilized to their maximum capacity when output is large. Consequently, the same high fixed costs are incurred regardless of the scale of production, which will result in the ATC being lowered for a firm with a larger scale of production.

When output increases, the high fixed costs from these indivisible factors are spread over a larger range of output and the firm is able to reap **technical economies of scale**, causing the LRAC curve to fall as output increases.

Natural Monopoly
A natural monopoly usually exists when there is **scope for economies of scale to be exploited over a very large range of output relative to the entire market demand.** Thus, a natural monopoly typically exists in industries where there is a high ratio of fixed to variable costs, as ATC will continue to decline when fixed costs are spread over higher levels of output.

Higher Barriers to Entry
Higher fixed costs can also serve as a barrier to entry. New firms are deterred from entering an industry with high startup costs (which also tend to be fixed costs), since they may lack the financial capital to invest in production or may be put off by the high risk of investment. As smaller firms are likely to produce at a smaller output than incumbent firms, they are unable to exploit significant internal economies of scale and will incur a higher average cost of production, preventing them from pricing their goods competitively. As a result, they are unlikely to enter the market, resulting in the monopoly power of the incumbent firms.

Long Run
In the long run, all factors are variable. This means that firms can choose their optimal scale of production and may even decide to increase their shop space, which could cause them to incur higher rental costs. Once the shop space has been committed, the higher rentals become a new fixed cost as the firm enters into a new short run phase.

24. Explain the use of Long Run Average Cost.

The **Long Run Average Cost** (LRAC) represents the **lowest possible average cost of production at each output level, in the long run when all factors of production** (except for the level of technology) **can be varied.**

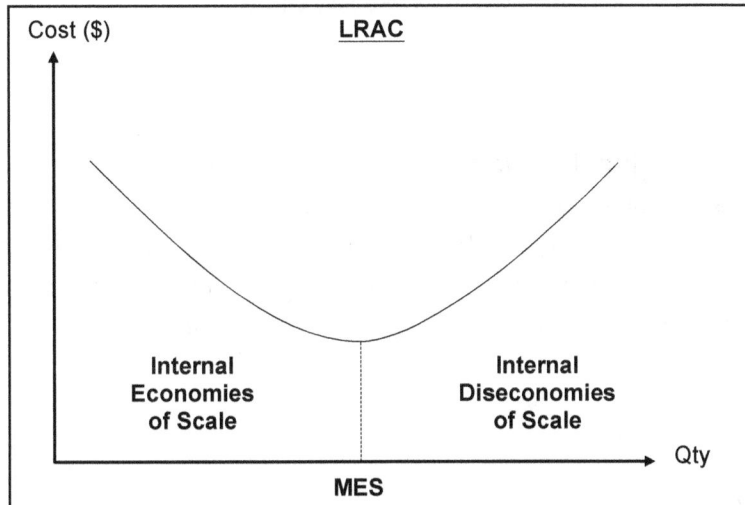

The LRAC is U-shaped. The falling part of the LRAC represents **internal economies of scale** while the rising part of the LRAC represents **internal diseconomies of scale.** Internal economies of scale are **cost savings,** which occur as the firm **increases its scale of production** while internal diseconomies of scale are **increases in average cost** which occur as the firm increases its scale of production.

The LRAC envelopes many **Short Run Average Cost** (SRAC) curves, each based on a particular fixed level of capital usage which represents a certain scale of production. The LRAC is tangential to these SRAC curves, as shown in the following diagram.

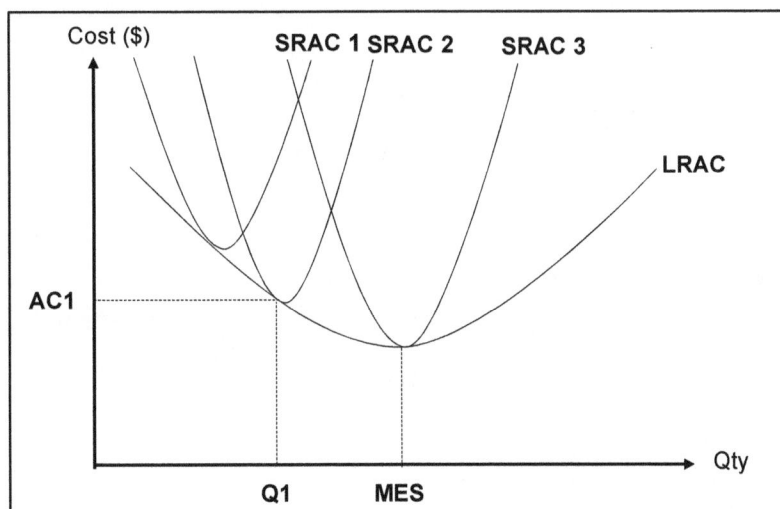

The LRAC is a **planning tool** which is useful in enabling firms to select the optimal scale of production based on the amount of output the firm expects to produce. For example, if the firm expects to produce Q1 amount of output, then the optimal scale of production would be the one that corresponds to SRAC 2. Although the firm can produce Q1 units of output even if it adopts other scales of production, represented by SRAC 1 and SRAC 3, it is the scale of production corresponding to SRAC 2 which will allow the firm to produce at the lowest AC of AC1.

Evaluation:

The LRAC can shift due to **changes in technology** as well as due to **external Economies of Scale.** For example, it can shift downwards if there are technological advancements or if the firm enjoys Economies of Concentration due to the clustering of firms from the same industry into the same geographical area. Such changes would cause the LRAC to fall at each and every output level.

25. Explain the use of the Minimum Efficient Scale (MES).

The **Minimum Efficient Scale** (MES) is the optimal firm size beyond which **no further internal economies of scale can be achieved.** It is the lowest level of output at which the lowest long run average costs are achieved. It is thus **the lowest point on the LRAC curve.** Beyond the MES, LRAC will begin to increase (except for saucer-shaped LRACs) due to internal diseconomies of scale.

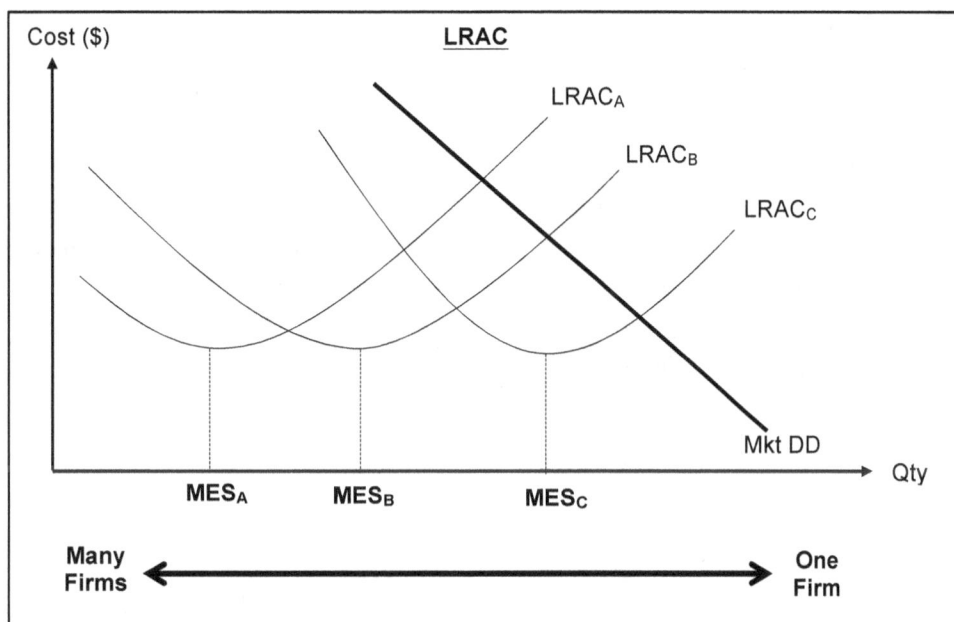

Knowledge of the MES is useful in predicting the number of firms in the industry and the relative size of these firms. When MES is considered relative to market demand, it also allows firms to gauge how much they should increase their scale of production to reap cost savings through internal economies of scale. If a firm increases output beyond the MES, it will run into internal diseconomies of scale which will cause Average Total Cost (ATC) to increase and subsequently, profits to decrease.

For example, in the diagram above, for the case of **LRAC$_A$**, it makes sense that there will be small firms in the industry as MES$_A$ occurs at a very low level of output, which means that even small firms can produce efficiently. Moreover, large firms will incur higher average costs due to diseconomies of scale. As the MES$_A$ is also very low relative to market demand, it is expected that there will be many small firms in this industry. Examples include hair salons and other personal services industries, which tend to fall under **monopolistic competition.**

Conversely, for the case of **LRAC$_C$**, it makes sense that there will be 1 large firm in the industry since the MES$_C$ occurs at a very large output level and is a very large fraction of the market demand. Such firms are typically known as **natural**

monopolies as there is scope for economies of scale to be exploited over a very large range of output relative to the entire market demand. Examples of such industries include Utilities such as water and gas supply.

In the case of $LRAC_B$, firms reach the MES_B at quite a large output level, which also represents quite a sizeable fraction of the market demand. As a result, there will tend to be a few large firms in this industry. Examples of such industries include automobile and pharmaceutical industries, which tend to be **oligopolistic** in nature.

Evaluation:

Saucer-shaped LRAC
It is possible for a saucer shaped LRAC (with a very large flat portion in the centre) to exist. There is a horizontal segment of the curve between the downward sloping and upward sloping portions, where the firm is experiencing constant returns to scale (CRTS). When this occurs, there are many different efficient scales of production, from Q_{MES} to Q1 as seen in the following diagram. In such a case, there is likely to be many firms of varying sizes in the industry. Examples include retailing and light manufacturing such as furniture making.

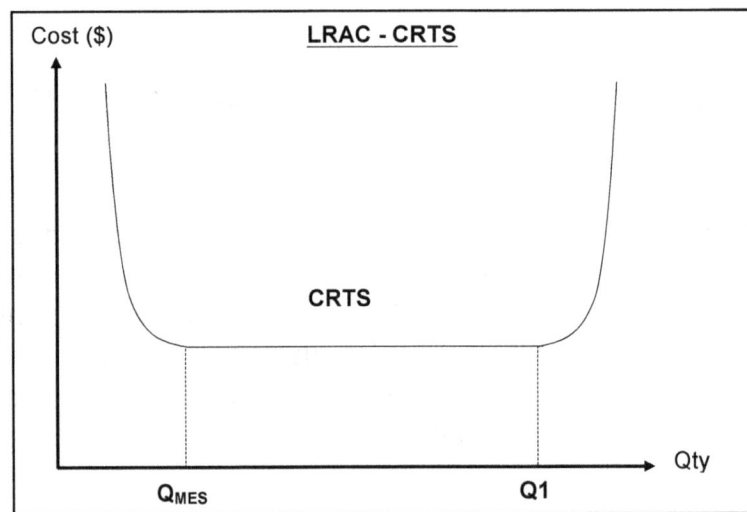

26. Explain the difference between internal economies of scale (iEOS) and external economies of scale (eEOS).

Point of Comparison	Internal Economies of Scale	External Economies of Scale
Definition	**Internal economies of scale** (iEOS) are **cost savings** enjoyed by a firm as a result of **the firm's expansion**, and have been created by the firm's own policies and actions.	**External economies of scale** (eEOS) are **cost savings** enjoyed by all firms as a result of an **expansion of the entire industry** or due to the **concentration of firms in a certain location.**
Diagrammatic representation	Represented by the falling part of the LRAC curve 	Represented by a downward shift of the entire LRAC curve, reducing the average cost at each level of output
Types and examples (3 examples of each)	**Technical iEOS** • **Economies due to specialization and division of labour:** As workers gain experience in specific areas of responsibility, productivity increases, and per unit cost of production falls. For example, in a restaurant, a single chef may initially handle cooking both main dishes and desserts while making basic food preparations. However, as the restaurant expands, the scale of production increases and it can afford to hire more chefs, each of which can specialise in cooking dishes of a certain	**Economies of Concentration** • These are cost savings that occur when firms are clustered in the same geographical area, thus benefiting in terms of the availability of better infrastructure and skilled labour. • **Infrastructure:** Better transport infrastructure, commercial facilities and public utilities can be built to cater to the needs of an industry when firms are closely located. In Singapore, during the development of the petrochemical industry on Jurong Island, roads were built to link firms on the island to the mainland, thereby enabling suppliers to transport

type. This reduces the time spent training chefs, while increasing their productivity in cooking each specific dish.

- **Factor indivisibility economies:** Certain factors of production (e.g. heavy machinery, infrastructure) are indivisible, which means they are only available in large sizes and therefore can only be effectively utilized when output is large. Examples include heavy machinery like harvesters. Such factors usually incur high fixed costs but as output increases, fixed costs are spread over a wider range of output, lowering average costs.

- **Economies due to increased dimensions:** Some factor inputs may be more efficient and help to lower costs simply because they are large. For example, firms' expansion may lead them to purchase larger containers to package and store their items. According to the Container Principle, as the size of a container increases, volume increases at a faster rate than surface area. This means that output increases at a faster rate than the cost of materials used to make the container. Thus, the cost of transporting each item decreases as output increases.

- **Linked process economies:** Large factories that can take a single good through multiple stages in its production can

raw materials to the plants and plants to transport finished products to distributors. Firms also share a jetty on Jurong Island, instead of having to build and maintain one each. This lowers their average costs significantly.

- **Skilled labour:** Special educational institutes and facilities can be set up to train people in industry-specific skills. For example, Silicon Valley, well known for housing many IT start-ups, also attracts many prestigious private educational institutions, increasing the ease of identifying and honing talent, which will be useful for the industry. This increases productivity and lowers the cost of employing and training labour.

help to minimize travelling and transport costs.	
Managerial iEOS • As the firm's scale of production increases, it may find it necessary to hire experts and specialists with specific skills, which can be employed in specific areas. For example, firms may hire more Human Resource (HR) and Finance Managers. • This allows specific managers to increase their experience within own spheres of responsibility, increasing their productivity and lowering average costs for the firm.	**Economies of Information** • Trade associations or central research institutions can publish trade journals or newsletters which helps to spread the cost of research and obtaining information over a larger number of firms.
Marketing iEOS • Larger firms have more market power, which in turn enables them to have greater bargaining power. They tend to buy supplies in bulk and are thus accorded preferential treatment (e.g. discounts) by suppliers. • Advertising costs, which are also fixed costs, can also be spread over a larger range of output. For example, newspaper advertisements for sushi takeaway service will be fixed regardless of the firm's scale of production and amount of sushi output produced. Therefore, as sushi output increases, the AFC of producing each sushi gradually falls as fixed costs are spread over a wider output.	**Economies of Disintegration** • The entire production process is split up and subsidiary industries are developed to produce goods for the major industry. • Subsidiary industries can produce on a larger scale of production and thus benefit from internal economies of scale, thereby lowering production costs. For example, in the automobile industry, different subsidiary industries have evolved to produce different parts of the car – internal combustion engines, leather seats, car tyres and so on. • This in turn means that automobile firms are able to lower their unit cost of production since these components can now be obtained more cheaply.

Evaluation:

Advantages of Small Firms

Even though it may seem advantageous for a firm to expand as much as possible in order to reap internal economies of scale, there are good reasons for small firms to exist as well. These include both supply- and demand-side factors. Some examples are listed below:

Supply-side factors:

- Firms can face increased costs due to **internal diseconomies of scale** once they increase output past the MES. Thus, if the firm reaches the MES at very low levels of output relative to market demand, it makes more sense for the firm to remain small.

- In industries where barriers to entry are low or non-existent, such as due to low start-up costs, many small firms are likely to exist.

- Small firms can **band together** to buy their supplies in bulk, enjoying benefits that are similar to the marketing iEOS which large firms enjoy, whilst retaining their independence.

Demand-side factors:

- Small firms may exist to cater to **niche markets** where there is limited demand for the goods catered by these firms. For example, specialized boutiques selling evening gowns operate on a smaller scale whereas mass market clothing brands tend to sell a wide variety of clothes and operate on a larger scale.

- In industries where **personalised attention** is required and each customer receives customised treatment, mass production by a large firm is not feasible and there are very limited internal economies of scale to be reaped. For example, tailors, doctors and dentists tend to operate on a smaller scale.

- Smaller firms may be more **nimble** in adapting to changes in demand conditions (such as changes in consumers' tastes and preferences) due to lower fixed costs and closer interactions with consumers as a result of more personalized services, This may prove advantageous in allowing them to respond to consumers' changing needs more rapidly and flexibly than larger firms.

27. Explain the different types of Mergers & Acquisitions (M&A).

Merger refers to the act of two or more firms **amalgamating to form a new enterprise**, while **acquisition** refers to **one firm buying over another**, in which the latter loses its identity completely.

There are 3 types of M&A – Vertical Integration, Horizontal Integration and Conglomeration.

Vertical Integration
Vertical integration takes place between two or more firms which are in the **same industry** but which are involved in **different stages of the production process**. There are 2 types of vertical integration: **backward integration** and **forward integration.**

In **forward integration**, the firm merges with firm(s) involved in **succeeding stages of production**. This enables the firm to **secure enough market outlets** and **control distribution lines**. An example would be a chocolate manufacturer who chooses to buy up retail outlets to sell his or her products. This in turn allows the firm to lower costs, as the need for workers to negotiate for distribution becomes redundant. It also brings the firm closer to the consumers, which can enable it to better understand tastes and preferences so that it can successfully practice product differentiation.

In **backward integration,** the firm merges with firm(s) involved in an **earlier stage of production**. This allows the firm to **secure raw materials** and have **greater control over their quantity and quality**. It also removes the need for workers to negotiate procurement and removes the intermediate profit margin, thereby cutting costs for the firm. An example would be an oil refinery, which buys up oil wells.

Lowering costs through vertical integration enables the firm to earn greater profits. It will also be able to lower its price, thereby increasing price-competitiveness which will allow it to sell more output and increase its market share by 'squeezing' out other firms in the market.

Horizontal Integration
Horizontal integration occurs when a firm merges with or acquires another firm **in the same industry, at the same stage of production.** For example, in Singapore, the United Overseas Bank (UOB) acquired the Overseas Union Bank (OUB) in 2001. The purpose of horizontal integration may be to expand operations and reap **greater internal economies of scale,** or to increase demand, revenue and market share by eliminating competitors.

Conglomeration

Conglomeration involves the combination of two or more firms in **different industries**. It enables firms to **diversify** their range of products so as to reduce the risk of fluctuations in demand, as losses in one sector can be offset by gains in another. Firms may also be able to gain cost advantages from increased economies of scope by producing a wider range of products. This allows the average total cost of production to fall as various overhead costs, such as the cost of Human Resource and Finance personnel can be shared amongst the various products. Similar inputs could also be used across the range of products, which means that bulk buying of these inputs will help lower unit costs across the range of products.

For example, a large conglomerate like Samsung can bulk buy electronic components needed for its large range of products, including cameras, LCD TVs, smartphones, printers and other products, thus achieving marketing economies of scale.

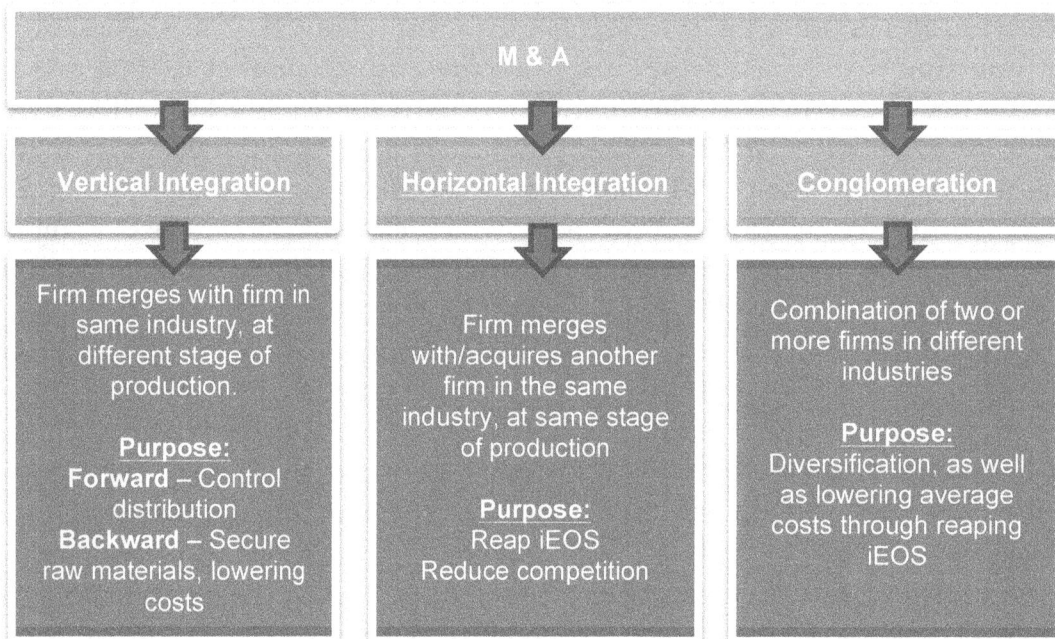

M & A		
Vertical Integration	**Horizontal Integration**	**Conglomeration**
Firm merges with firm in same industry, at different stage of production. **Purpose:** **Forward** – Control distribution **Backward** – Secure raw materials, lowering costs	Firm merges with/acquires another firm in the same industry, at same stage of production **Purpose:** Reap iEOS Reduce competition	Combination of two or more firms in different industries **Purpose:** Diversification, as well as lowering average costs through reaping iEOS

28. Explain possible advantages and disadvantages of M&A.

The effects of mergers and acquisitions should be evaluated in terms of **cost and revenue advantages and disadvantages.**

A. Cost advantages

Internal Economies of Scale
Larger firms are able to reap **internal economies of scale (see Question 26)**, which will enable them to reap cost savings. This is reflected by the movement along the LRAC curve from A to B, which is closer to the MES, as shown in the diagram below.

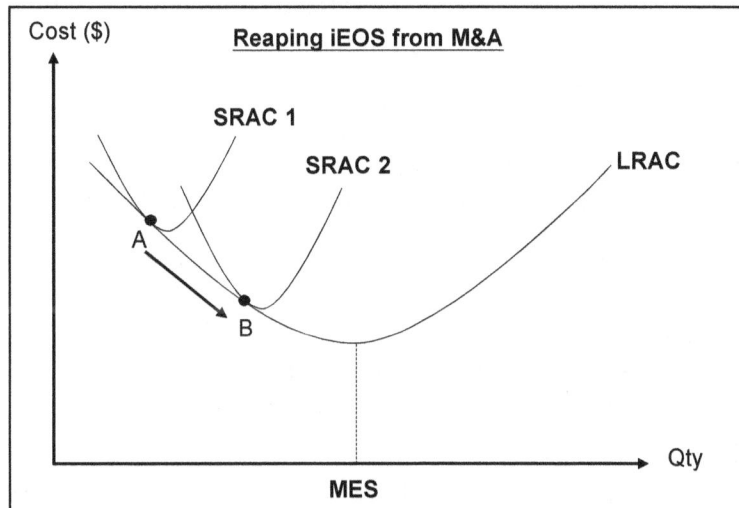

This is also reflected by a downward diagonal shift of **both the MC and the SRAC** along the LRAC, as shown in the following diagram. This can enable them to earn higher profits and price more competitively, allowing them to capture market share as seen in the following diagram.

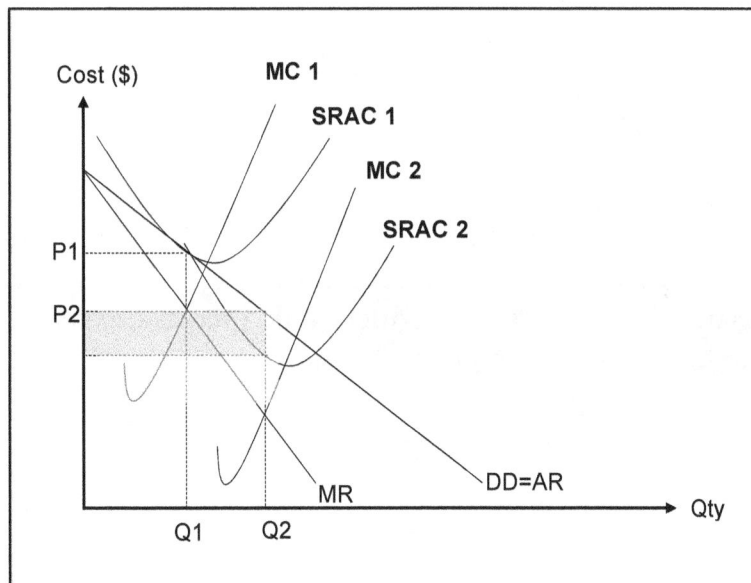

At the initial profit maximizing equilibrium (P1,Q1) where MC1=MR, the firm was earning Normal profits as the AR=AC. As a result of the merger or acquisition, there is now a larger firm reaping iEOS and therefore experiencing both a lower MC and SRAC at MC2 and SRAC2 respectively. This has enabled the firm to price more competitively and also earn supernormal profits as seen in the new profit maximizing equilibrium (P2, Q2), where the AR is now > AC.

Remove Duplication

In addition, integration with other firms will allow them to **remove duplication** by merging similar operations carried out by different firms, and streamlining the production process. For example, it reduces the need for two different finance departments and they can be consolidated, saving manpower and other administrative costs. This will enable firms to lower the per unit cost of production.

Lower advertising costs

M&A can also reduce the need for firms to advertise, as there is one less competitor for the firm to compete against for the consumers' attention. This lowers advertising costs.

R&D and Technology

Firms may be able to leverage on the other firm's technology to improve and streamline production processes, lowering the cost of production.

Moreover, by lowering per unit costs through the internal economies of scale and increasing revenue, M&A will enable firms to earn greater profits, which they can use to **invest in R&D and advanced technology**. If successful, this can in turn further lower costs and increase revenue.

M&A also lowers the per unit costs of R&D, since R&D entails fixed costs which will now be spread over a larger range of output. This increases the profitability of R&D investments.

B. Revenue advantages

Increased Demand

As M&A reduces the number of rivals in the market, it **helps to increase the market share** of the firms involved. As a result, assuming total market demand remains constant, **demand for the firm's products will increase**, ceteris paribus. This will enable the firm to benefit from higher revenue.

More Price-Inelastic Demand

In addition, as the number of competitors in the market decreases, fewer substitutes become available and thus, **demand for the firm's products becomes more price-inelastic** (as shown in the following diagram). This increases their market power and gives firms greater leeway to increase revenue by raising prices.

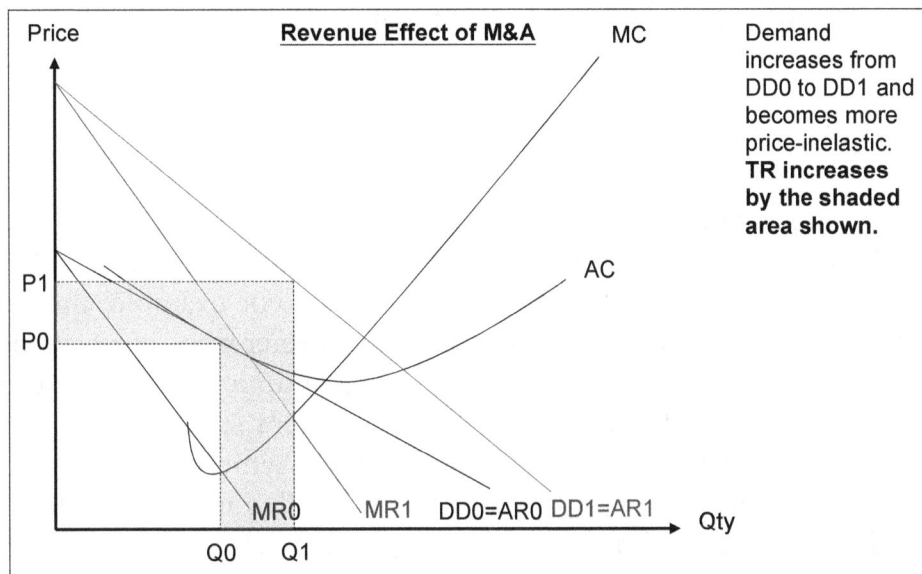

R&D and Technology

By lowering costs and increasing revenue, M&A will enable firms to earn **greater profits** which they can use to **invest** in **R&D and improved technology**. This may allow them to differentiate their products further, increasing demand for their products.

C. Cost disadvantages

Internal Diseconomies of Scale

When a firm merges with or acquires another firm, its scale of production increases and it produces a larger output. As a result, the firm may run into **internal diseconomies of scale,** which are increases in the average cost of production as a result of the firm's expansion. For example, monitoring costs may increase as it may be harder to **coordinate** between different departments of the firm. Furthermore, the decision-making process may be slow and inefficient due to the long chain of authority, leading to time lags and lack of **communication** between different parties. This is because of the larger size of the organization with many different departments each specialising in separate areas. Relationships may also become strained as employees may feel alienated by the firm's management, given that the organisation is larger and there are more levels of hierarchy within the firm. This could lead to poor work attitudes and lower productivity, increasing the per unit cost of production.

The merger of two distinct, separate firms may potentially result in conflicts and clashes in management styles and culture, leading to control problems. This will lower productivity significantly, offsetting the benefits of a merger. A well-known example of a merger that failed due to this reason would be that between automotive producers Daimler and Chrysler. Daimler was a German company which valued hierarchy and respect, and prided itself on creating high-quality, efficient and safe products, while Chrysler was an American company which relied on creativity and daring to gain an edge in the market. Ultimately, culture clashes between the two firms caused the merger to fall apart.

D. Revenue disadvantages

Inflexibility and Loss of Focus
M&A tends to result in larger firms that may find it more difficult to adapt and respond to changes in demand/market conditions. For example, they may find it difficult to respond to changes in the tastes and preferences of consumers. This is likely due to the same problem of a lack of communication and coordination as discussed earlier. In addition, conflicts in management styles and cultures can also lead to the firm losing focus and becoming unsure of which market segment to focus on, which may negatively impact product quality. This may cause demand for the firm's products to fall, leading to a fall in revenue. Such internal conflicts may also distract firms from focusing on increasing market share as it spends time ironing out differences instead.

An example would be the Power Sybase acquisition of Powersoft. While the former focused on producing database software, the latter focused on software development tools and the firm struggled to determine what its core focus should be and ended up losing market share.

Evaluation:

Government Regulation
Mergers may not always be feasible as they may be prohibited by legislation or prevented by the competition commission/authorities, to avoid the creation of firms with excessive monopoly power. Quite recently, the European antitrust regulators blocked the merger of UPS and TNT Express, 2 large international package delivery companies. Likewise, the Competition Commission of Singapore (CCS) disallows mergers under the Competition Act if they substantially lessen competition or distort it. Exceptions may be made if the proposed merger results in economic efficiencies, greater innovation or choice, higher quality and lower costs.

Mergers: Failure or Success?
Most mergers seem to fail. According to McKinsey reports, while 80% of mergers are done for revenue reasons, only 12% actually result in increased revenues.

M & A Advantages/Disadvantages			

Advantages		Disadvantages	

COST	REVENUE	COST	REVENUE
• Internal EOS • Remove duplication • Lower advertising costs	• Increased DD • More price-inelastic DD • Increased market power	• Internal disEOS • Differences in culture/ management style	• Inflexibility • Loss of focus

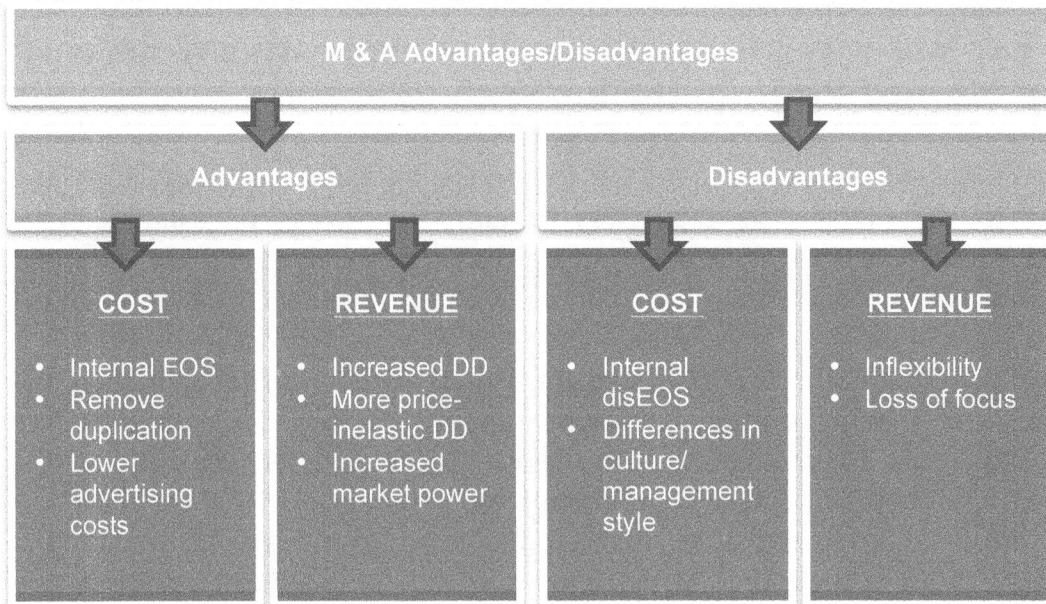

Remember '3 Cs' when discussing diseconomies of scale: Costs arising from the lack of **communication, coordination and control** as the firm expands.

29. Explain why Monopolistically Competitive firms only earn Normal Profit in the long run.

In monopolistically competitive (MPC) markets, there is a relatively large number of firms in the industry and **barriers to entry are low**. For example, factors of production are fairly mobile, and start-up costs (such as rental costs and capital costs) are low.

When an MPC firm makes **short-run supernormal profits**, new firms will be attracted to the industry. Since barriers to entry are low, they can easily enter the industry. Assuming market demand remains unchanged, the entry of new firms into the MPC market will cause the **demand** for the individual firms' products to **fall** from DD0 to DD1 as customers are diverted away from existing firms. Demand also becomes **more price-elastic** as the number of substitutes increases. As a result, the profit maximizing equilibrium changes from E0 (where MR0 = MC) to E1 (where MR1 = MC). This leads to the loss of revenue represented by the shaded area in the diagram as **new firms will continue to enter the market until all supernormal profits are eroded.** At the new profit-maximising equilibrium E1, AR = AC and the MPC firm is now earning normal profits.

Thus, MPC firms can only earn normal profits in the long run.

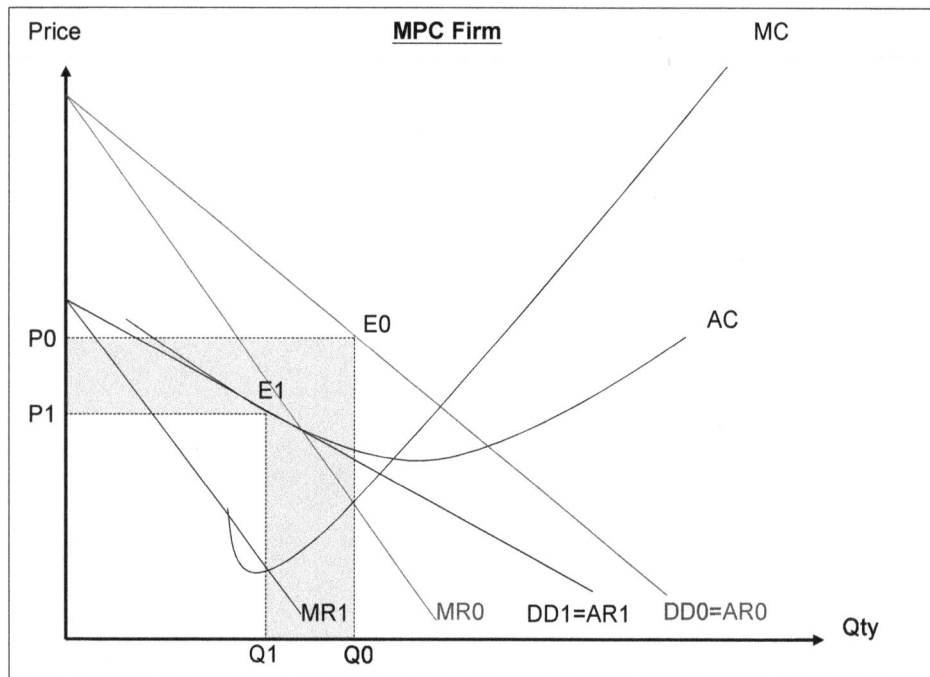

30. Explain why a Monopoly may be preferred over Perfect Competition.

A. Consumer Welfare

<u>Lower Price & Higher Quantity (Greater Consumer Surplus)</u>
In a monopoly, consumers may benefit from a **lower price** and a **larger output** than in a PC market, resulting in increased **consumer surplus**. This is due to the ability of the monopoly to **reap significant internal economies of scale**.

As the monopolist produces a much larger output and thus operates on a much larger scale of production than the PC firm, it can exploit internal economies of scale which will allow it to **lower its per unit cost of production**, causing its **Marginal Cost (MC) curve to be lower than the PC market supply curve**. As such, at the profit-maximising output level where MR = MC (where MC is increasing), the monopolist may price its product at P2, which is lower than the market price of P1 as in the case of the PC market. Furthermore, output also increases from Q1 to Q2.

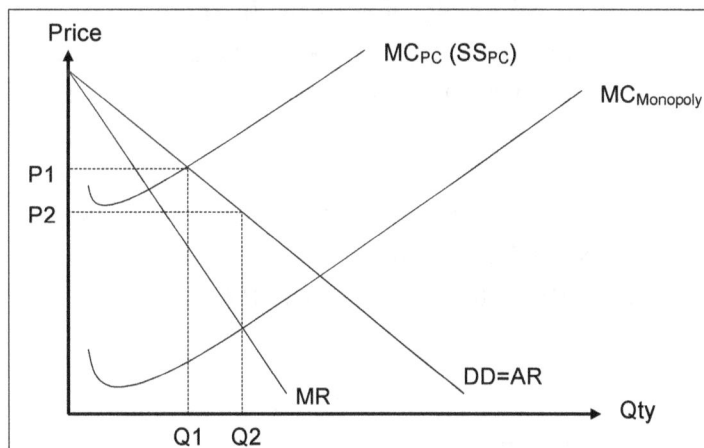

<u>Quality of Product and Technological Advancement</u>
As monopolists are able to make supernormal profits in the long run due to high barriers to entry, they possess the ability to **engage in R&D and product innovation** which will allow them to enhance the quality of existing products. They can also discover improved production methods which may reduce the cost of production and subsequently, prices, improving consumer welfare.

However, a PC market has no barriers to entry and thus, PC firms can only make **normal profits in the long run.** They **lack the ability** to carry out R&D to improve product quality. Furthermore, it has no incentive to do so since it is assumed that all products are **homogeneous** (identical to one another) and any innovation can be **easily replicated** by rival firms, due to the assumption of perfect information. Thus, the monopolist is more dynamically efficient than the PC firms.

Consumer Choice

Although consumers will not be able to choose which producer to purchase goods from in a monopoly, they could benefit from **greater product range.** The monopolist may **practice product and brand proliferation,** enabling consumers to benefit from increased choice and variety in order to deter potential entrants from entering the market. This is especially the case when the market is a **contestable** one which faces the threat of potential entrants.

On the other hand, in a PC market, consumers are able to choose from a large number of producers, but **as all products are perfectly homogeneous,** the consumers have no choice in terms of the products on sale.

Product Availability

Furthermore, price discrimination enables monopolists to produce goods, which may otherwise not be produced due to high costs, thus increasing **product availability**. This is especially important for industries with high fixed costs due to extensive capital equipment required yet experience low levels of demand for their products, such that the average cost of production is higher than the price that consumers are willing and able to pay at all levels of output. In the case of a perfectly competitive market, the good would not be produced as the price is always below the firm's AC. As a result, all the PC firms would be earning subnormal profits, leading them to exit the market.

Without price discrimination, the market would not exist as firms would make economic losses. With perfect price discrimination, however, the monopolist may be profitable, depending on the relative sizes of FHD and GEC as shown in the diagram below.

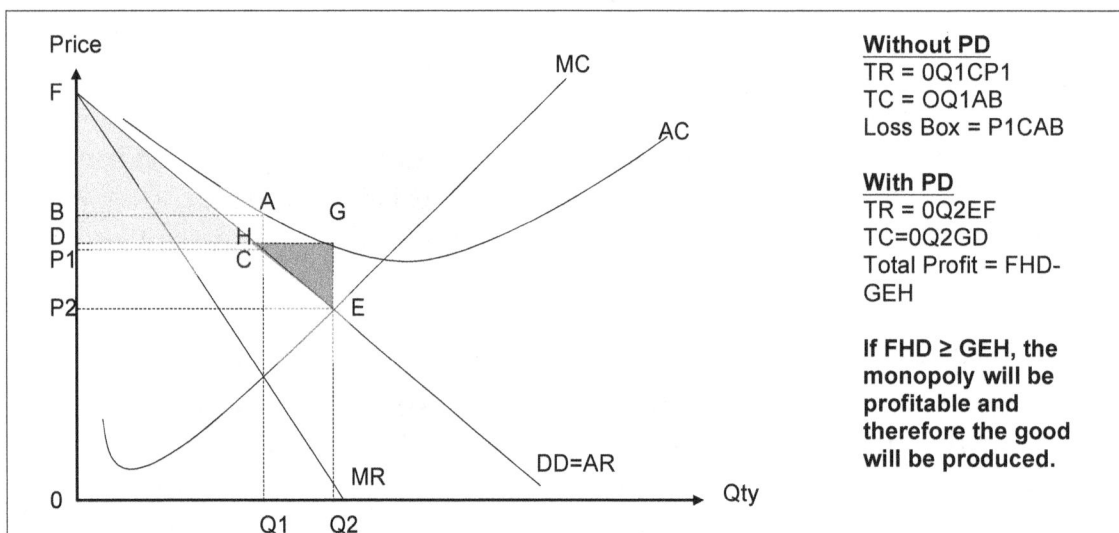

Without PD
TR = 0Q1CP1
TC = 0Q1AB
Loss Box = P1CAB

With PD
TR = 0Q2EF
TC=0Q2GD
Total Profit = FHD-GEH

If FHD ≥ GEH, the monopoly will be profitable and therefore the good will be produced.

Evaluation:

Government Policies to regulate Price and Output
Although the monopolist usually produces at a higher price and a lower output than the PC firm, government policies such as MC and AC pricing can help to reduce price and increase output, thus increasing consumer surplus and equity whilst addressing allocative inefficiency. This is especially so in the case of a natural monopoly where due to the huge internal economies of scale, it makes more sense to have only one firm serving the entire market. By allowing the monopoly to exist whilst regulating its price and output through government policies, society will be able to benefit from the advantages of a monopoly, while minimising its disadvantages.

In summary, benefits tend to be greater when:
- There are substantial iEOS to be reaped
- The market is contestable

Tip

Note that it is not possible to compare a perfectly competitive firm with a monopoly firm. It is only possible to compare a perfectly competitive **market** with a monopoly market.

To illustrate this, start off with a PC market (a usual demand-supply diagram), and then draw an MR curve with double the slope of the demand curve to represent the monopolized market. The monopoly's MC curve may also be represented as the supply curve of the PC market.

31. Explain why MC=MR is the profit maximising condition.

All firms are assumed to be **profit-maximising**, which means that they aim to earn the highest possible amount of total profits. In order to maximise profits, firms produce at the output level where **MC=MR, and MC is rising**. The firm will produce up to the level where the additional revenue earned from the last unit sold, i.e. marginal revenue (MR) is equivalent to the additional cost of producing it, i.e. marginal cost (MC). This is also known as the **marginalist principle**.

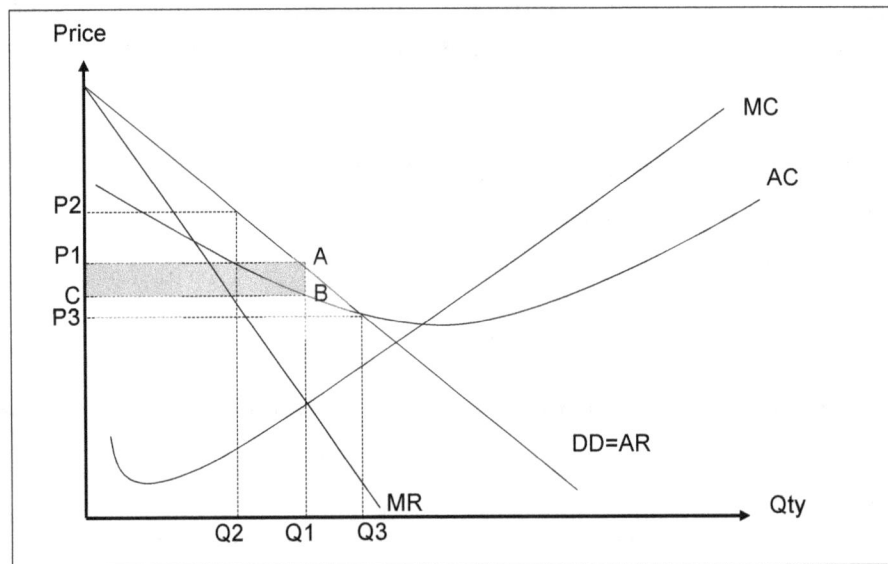

At Q2, since MR > MC, **the additional TR earned from the last unit of output sold is greater than the additional cost incurred from its production**. Thus, the firm can increase its total profits if it increases production. **Profits are not maximized when MR > MC.**

At Q3, however, since MR < MC, this means that the sale of the last unit of output adds less to TR than the additional cost incurred from its production. Thus, the last unit of output produced will result in a fall in total profits. The firm can increase its total profits if it decreases its level of production, and **profits are not maximized when MR < MC.**

Hence, at Q1 where MR = MC and at P1, the firm is able to maximise profits and its total profits are measured as the area P1ABC.

32. Explain how R&D as well as advertising and branding can be a form of barrier to entry (BTE).

In some industries, R&D may be necessary in product development and a firm cannot successfully compete if it lacks the financial or technological capabilities to carry out such R&D. An example of such an industry would be the smartphone industry where better products are launched almost on a yearly basis. In addition, in imperfect markets especially oligopolies, existing firms tend to engage in heavy advertising and branding which is seen as a non-pricing strategy to differentiate its products from its rivals', increase consumer awareness of its product and build brand loyalty.

As a result, new entrants who are unable to carry out R&D and advertising on the same scale may fail to compete with incumbent firms. Yet these often entail **heavy startup costs,** which new firms are unlikely to be able to afford and also they do not enjoy the benefits of internal economies of scale when producing at an initial low output. Thus, extensive R&D, advertising and branding serve as a **barrier to entry** since new entrants lack the financial capital or may be put off by the high risk of investment.

33. Explain how IEOS is a form of BTE.

In industries where there are significant internal economies of scale to be exploited, such as in the case of a **natural monopoly**, incumbent firms which are already operating on a larger scale are able to enjoy significant cost advantage and produce at a lower unit cost of production. For example, if there is a high ratio of fixed to variable costs, average costs will continue to fall as output increases.

New entrants, however, will begin operation on a smaller scale and incur a higher average cost of production. As shown in the following diagram, the SRAC and MC of the incumbent firm (represented by SRAC 2 and MC 2 respectively) will be lower than that of the startup firm (represented by SRAC 1 and MC 1 respectively).

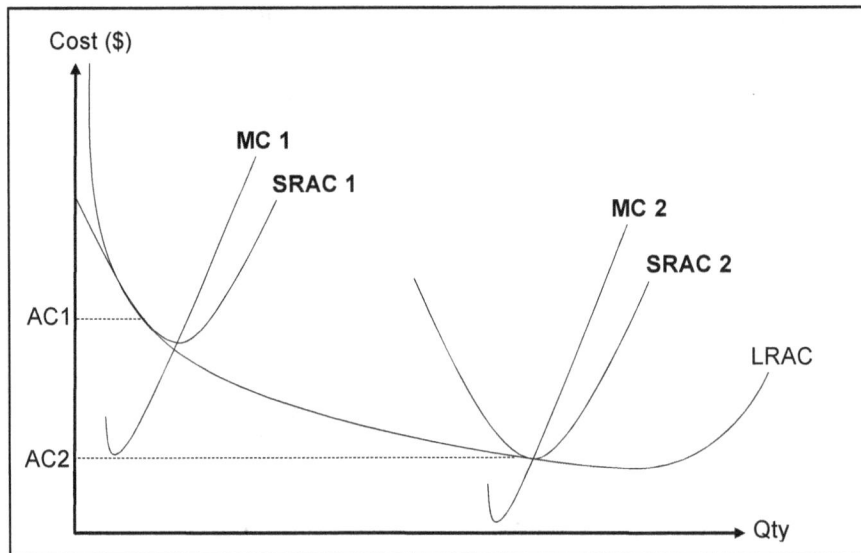

Thus, as illustrated in the following diagram, startup firms will not be able to price as competitively as incumbents and **cannot compete effectively** with them. This discourages new entrants from entering the market since it is likely to be unprofitable for them to do so, thereby serving as a **barrier to entry**.

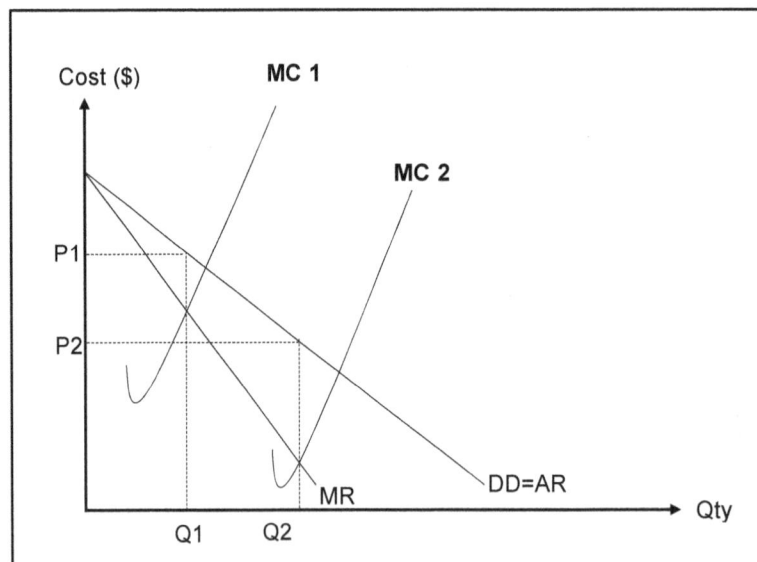

Evaluation:

<u>Strategic barriers to entry</u>
Firms which enjoy significant iEOS are also often in a better position to erect **strategic barriers to entry** which will further ward off potential entrants, since they often have **greater supernormal profits** which places them in a better position to carry out **predatory pricing, R&D** as well as **takeovers and acquisitions.** For example, they can intentionally lower their prices below the MC to squeeze rivals out of the market, sustaining losses in the short run with the knowledge that it can recoup them once competition has been forced to exit the market.

34. Explain why non-price strategies may or may not benefit society.

Non-price strategies include **product differentiation, branding and advertising,** as well as **R&D** to develop and innovate new products, and improve the existing range of products. Non-price strategies are primarily carried out in imperfect markets such as monopolistically competitive markets, monopolies, and especially **oligopolies**. While non-price strategies tend to benefit societies in terms of **consumer choice and welfare, dynamic efficiency** and **increased competition,** they may also lead to **allocative inefficiency** due to wasteful duplication, exacerbate the problem of **imperfect information**, and may **decrease the level of competition in the market** by serving as a barrier to entry.

Benefit society	Will not benefit society
Consumer Choice and Welfare • Non-price strategies such as **product differentiation** through product development and innovation can help to increase **product range and quality**. • For example, improving the quality of ingredients used in a hawker stall can help to improve consumer welfare, as consumers benefit from better quality food. • In addition, developing new products can allow consumers to benefit from a wider range of products, improving **consumer choice.** For example, Samsung offers a wide variety of smartphones with different sizes and functionalities. • **Advertising** which is a non-price strategy can potentially provide consumers with useful and reliable information about the product which will enable consumers to make informed decisions.	**Allocative Inefficiency** • Engaging in large-scale advertising or R&D efforts which do not yield results may be perceived to be a misallocation of resources, as resources (e.g. capital) are spent on non-productive uses such as marketing, rather than on increasing output. • Non-price strategies may also lead to wasteful duplication of other firms' R&D efforts.

Dynamic Efficiency	Imperfect Information
• Dynamic efficiency is concerned with technological advancements and innovation over time. Therefore non-price strategies like R&D to develop better quality products will help to improve dynamic efficiency.	• **Misleading** advertising may also worsen imperfect information if it oversells product benefits, leading to over-consumption and market failure.
Greater competition	**Lower competition**
• Engaging in non-price strategies such as extensive advertising and marketing can help to spur competition in a market as rivals' products become more visible to consumers, effectively increasing the range of firms which consumers can choose to purchase from. • This may in turn spur price competition, or more R&D and innovation to develop better products.	• Non-price strategies such as extensive advertising and R&D may be considered **barriers to entry**, since they effectively deter new entrants who are unable to innovate or advertise on the same scale when they enter the market. • This may have the effect of lowering the level of competition in the market, which may have other adverse impacts on economic efficiency and societal welfare.

35. Explain Mutual Interdependence.

Mutual interdependence is a key characteristic of oligopolies. In oligopolies, the market is dominated by a few firms each controlling significant market share. As a result, each firm's actions will have significant impact on rival firms and vice versa. This leads to a strong degree of rivalry between firms, which means that they will **closely monitor actions of rival firms**, and will also **anticipate their reactions** before deciding to implement any price or non-price strategy.

Due to mutual interdependence, oligopolistic firms will tend to **avoid price-competition**, and **pursue non-price competition** instead (see Question 36). They may also choose to collude, since by doing so, the actions of all firms would be jointly agreed upon, minimising the unpredictability of rivals' actions.

Tip

Why don't monopolistically competitive firms exhibit mutual interdependence?
In a monopolistically competitive market, many small firms exist, each with very limited market share. As such, the action of any one firm will have practically no impact on other firms. An example would be that of chicken rice stalls in Singapore: Out of the thousands of chicken rice stalls, if one chicken rice stall lowers its price, chicken rice stalls in other parts of Singapore are unlikely to be significantly impacted by the price change. However, an exception would be chicken rice stalls in very close proximity, such as chicken rice stalls that exist within the same hawker centre. In such instances, if one chicken rice stall lowers its price, the other chicken rice stalls in the hawker centre are likely to be adversely impacted. These chicken rice stalls may be regarded as firms existing within a localised oligopoly.

36. Why does price rigidity occur for Oligopolies?

As oligopolies only consist of a few dominant firms, it is likely that firms will be impacted by rivals' pricing strategies and will respond to such changes accordingly. **As such, each firm will assess or predict its rivals' reactions to its pricing strategies.** This gives rise to the kinked demand curve theory, which follows from the mutual interdependence experienced by oligopolistic firms.

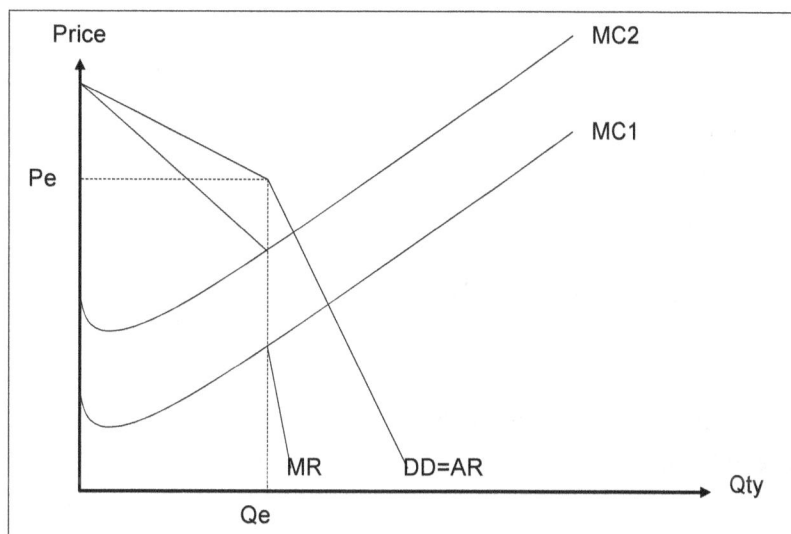

If a firm raises its price **above** the prevailing market price Pe, the firm assesses that rival firms are unlikely to follow since they would be able to gain market share by maintaining their current price. As a result, when the price is raised above Pe, quantity demanded for the firm's product will fall more than proportionately to the price increase, implying a **price-elastic demand above Pe.** Hence, **total revenue will fall** when the price is raised.

Conversely, if the firm lowers its price **below** the equilibrium price Pe, it assesses that rivals are likely to match its price reduction so as not to lose market share. Thus, quantity demanded for the firm's product will increase less than proportionately to the reduction in price. This implies a **price-inelastic demand below Pe** and **total revenue will fall** when the price is lowered.

Thus, the DD = AR curve is **kinked** and the MR curve is **discontinuous**. Since total revenue falls when price is raised and/or lowered, **the firm will avoid raising or lowering prices**, which leads to price rigidity.

Moreover, even if MC changes from MC 1 to MC 2 as shown in the diagram above, as long as it remains within the discontinuous region of MR below the kink, the profit-maximising equilibrium (where MC=MR) is still the same at PeQe. Hence, even if costs change, prices are likely to remain rigid. The firm will have to absorb the higher costs instead of passing it on to consumers in the form of higher prices, leaving the existing price-output combination unchanged.

Evaluation:

Price War
Oligopolistic firms do not generally engage in price-competition, since these usually escalate into price wars which tend to result in **lower revenue** and thus, **lower profits** for all in the short run.

However, oligopolistic firms sometimes initiate price wars, especially when there is considerable excess capacity in the market. Firms may regard price wars as an opportunity to squeeze out rival firms which cannot survive the price war. In order to retain market share and profitability, rival firms are forced to decrease prices as well, leading to a price war. However, lowering prices may lead to lower TR for these firms, which may cause them to make subnormal profits and be forced out of business in the long run.

Firms that produce closest to the MES (and thus at the lowest AC) are usually in the **best position to initiate a price cut** since they already enjoy lower unit costs than the other firms, allowing them to cut prices substantially without suffering huge losses. In addition, such firms are also likely to have earned more supernormal profits. These excess profits may serve as reserve funds, which the firms can tap into, allowing them to survive through a period of subnormal profits due to a price war.

37. Explain the types of collusion.

Collusion is a formal or informal agreement, typically between oligopolistic firms, on what prices to charge and how to divide the market. This helps to reduce the unpredictability of rivals' actions and increase the profits of the group as a whole, enabling them to **maximise joint profits.**

There are two main types of collusion: **a) tacit collusion**, an **informal agreement** in which the rules of collusive behaviour are unwritten, as well as **b) overt/explicit price-fixing,** in which a **formal agreement** is made regarding what prices to charge or how to divide the market.

Tacit Collusion
One form of tacit collusion is **price leadership** in which prices and price changes are established by a **dominant firm** which is regarded as the **price leader**. The price leader usually enjoys the most **internal economies of scale** and is able to produce at the **lowest average cost.** When the price leader initiates a change in price, other firms in the industry will adopt these price changes as doing so is accepted as the most ideal way to protect or increase their profits.

For example, when a petrol retailer which is a price leader increases its price, the other firms which experience higher average cost will eagerly follow suit as they can now raise prices to increase their profits.

Arguably, another example would be the leading taxi company in Singapore, Comfort Delgro, signaling to other taxi companies to follow its fare structure.

Overt Price-Fixing
Formal collusive agreements such as **cartels** typically involve limiting competition between member firms through agreed output quotas, limiting advertising (so as to reduce each firm's costs without fear of losing market share), agreeing not to poach each others' markets, and fixing prices. The purpose of explicit price-fixing is typically to maximise the joint profits of all member firms.

For example, in a cartel such as the Organisation of Petroleum Exporting Countries (**OPEC**), firms formally collude to set a fixed high price by restricting industry output. Each firm is given a fixed production quota, which they must keep to in order to restrict market supply and keep prices high, allowing them to maximise joint profits.

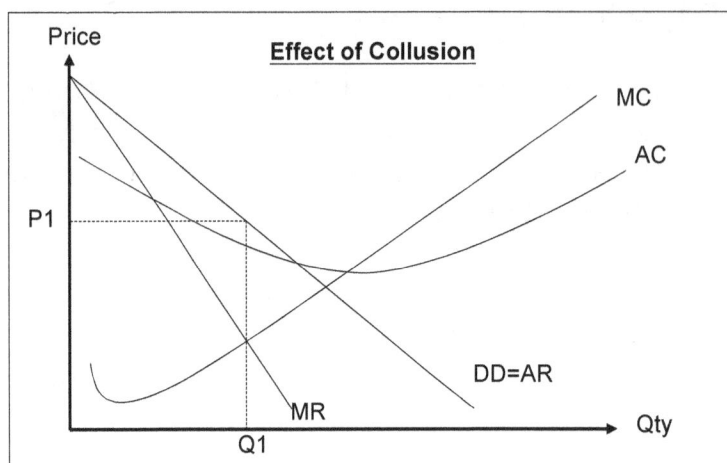

Since the firms have formed a cartel, they essentially function as a **joint monopoly**, and the monopoly demand curve is also equivalent to the market demand curve. As shown in the diagram above, the firms would essentially be functioning like a monopoly in which the industry output is restricted at Q1 and allocated across different firms, keeping the market price high at P1.

Evaluation:

Legality
Price-fixing is usually illegal, as Competition Laws usually enforce against it. Market regulators such as the US Office of Fair Trading and the Competition Commission of Singapore (CCS) disallow collusive agreements as they tend to worsen equity by enabling firms to exploit consumer welfare. For example, the Competition Commission of Singapore found the modelling association of Singapore guilty of encouraging price-fixing, and 11 modelling agencies were eventually fined for fixing the wages of models.

Uncertainty of Agreements
Collusive agreements are usually fragile, as members have strong incentive to cheat by increasing output beyond their stipulated quotas since doing so will allow them to earn extra profits. However, when various firms do so, there will be excess supply in the market, leading to a downward pressure on prices as firms will be forced to cut prices to clear the excess supply. The fall in prices lowers TR for all firms involved, eventually leading to the collapse of the price-fixing agreement.

Barriers to Collusion
- **Unstable demand conditions:** This may create excess capacity in the industry and places pressure on individual firms to lower prices to maintain profitability.
- **New entrants:** Non-cartel firms entering the market may cause the cartel to lose control of market price and output. This is likely due to falling **barriers to**

entry, perhaps as a result of advancements in technology. The increased competition will erode the market power of the cartel members and exert downward pressure on prices (due to falling demand) leading to the collapse of the price fixing agreement.

- **Enforcement problems:** The tendency to 'cheat' on collusive agreements is high, particularly if it is difficult to detect and prevent price cuts by member firms.

- **Differences in product:** The more differentiated the products, the harder it is to agree on a fixed price and also to maintain the collusion. The more differentiated their products, the more differences between their demand curves, increasing the difficulties to agree on a common price. For example, a firm whose product may possess some unique features may find it more beneficial to be charging a higher price than other firms, as the demand it faces is more price-inelastic, and a higher price can enable it to earn higher revenues. In addition, firms that have successfully differentiated its products may now believe that they can earn higher profits by competing against instead of colluding with rival firms, and therefore an existing collusive agreement may collapse.

- **Differences in cost conditions:** This may lead to disputes over the fixed price and how to allocate output among the firms. This is because firms with lower average costs can earn higher profits while firms with higher average costs will earn lower profits.

38. Explain X-Inefficiency.

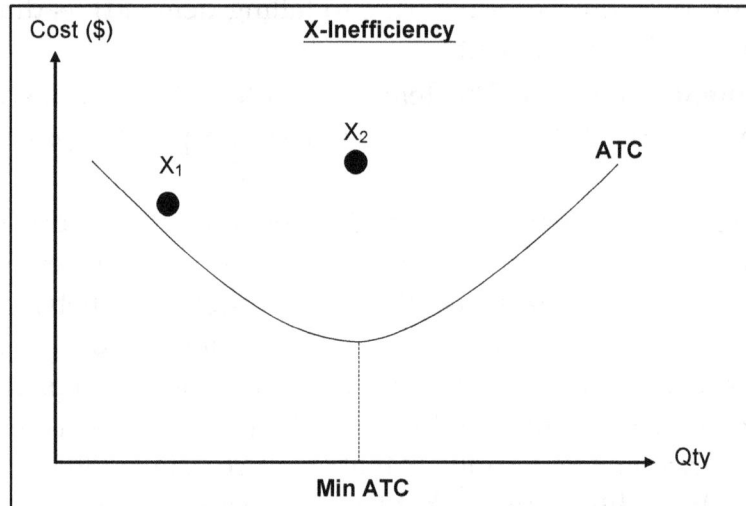

A firm which is **X-inefficient** is productively inefficient from the firm's and society's point of view as it is producing at a point **above** the average total cost (ATC) curve. For example, both points X_1 and X_2 in the diagram above show that the firm is X-inefficient. Since all the points on the ATC curve represent the lowest possible average cost of producing various levels of output (for a given scale of production), this means that firms operating at any point above the ATC are incurring more costs than necessary. For example, the firm may experience **organisational slack**, such as by overstaffing (employing more workers than is required).

In theory, only **oligopolistic** and **monopolistic** firms **can afford to be X-inefficient**. This is a result of **high barriers to entry**, which lead to a **lack of competition**, enabling the firms to retain their **supernormal profits** in the long run. The large supernormal profits earned tend to breed complacency and due to a lack of competition, the firms expect to earn supernormal profits even though they are X-inefficient. Conversely, firms in perfectly competitive and monopolistically competitive markets have low or no barriers to entry and can only make normal profits in the long run. Thus, they cannot afford to be X-inefficient or they will make losses and be eliminated from the market in the long run.

Once a firm is X-inefficient, it is also considered to be **productively-inefficient** since it is not even producing at a point along the ATC curve.

39. Explain productive efficiency.

Productive efficiency is a type of **economic efficiency**. It is defined as using resources to produce a good or service in the least cost manner.

MICRO

At the micro level, productive efficiency can be evaluated from **the firm's point of view** and from **society's point of view**.

Firm's POV

From the firm's point of view, all the points on the Average Total Cost (ATC) curve are productively efficient, because the ATC represents the lowest possible cost of production at each given level of output. A firm which produces at a point above the ATC is said to be **X-inefficient (see Question 38)**.

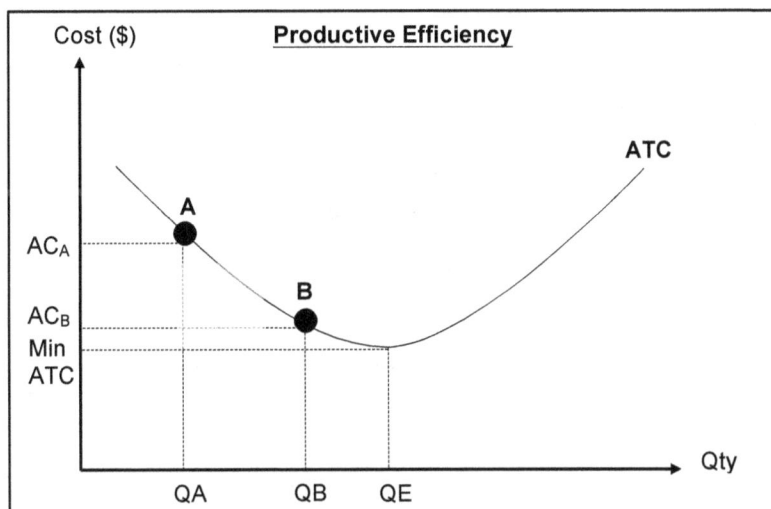

For example, both points A and B in the diagram above are productively efficient from the firm's viewpoint. To produce QA, A represents the lowest possible average cost at AC_A. Likewise, to produce QB, B represents the lowest possible average cost at AC_B.

Society's POV

From society's point of view, productive efficiency occurs at the **lowest AC**, which is the minimum point of the ATC curve, as seen in the diagram above. QE is therefore regarded as the productively efficient level of output from societal viewpoint. This means that the firm is making the best use of its available resources to produce the good at lowest per unit cost possible, given its current scale of production.

Macro Link:

At the macro level, productive efficiency is achieved when a country is producing the maximum output possible with its given resources and technology. Thus, production on **any point along the frontier** of the Production Possibility Curve (**PPC**) is productively efficient. Any point below the PPC means that the economy is not making the best use of its available resources.

Evaluation:

However, only one point on the PPC is allocatively efficient, as that is when the combination of goods maximises societal welfare.

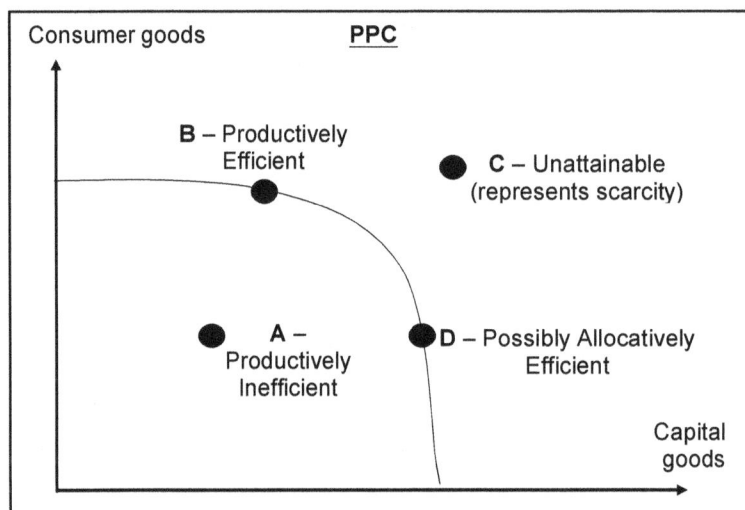

40. Explain how the different types of profit (subnormal, supernormal and normal) may be arrived at as a result of:
a. R&D investments in production technique
b. Increased fixed cost
c. Reduced demand

In the **long run**, only oligopolists and monopolists are able to make supernormal profits. However, in the **short run**, firms in any type of market structure are able to make **subnormal, normal and supernormal** profits.

a. R&D investments in production technique

In the **short run**, investment in technology incurs a **fixed cost** which causes the SRATC curve of the firm to shift upwards (SRATC = AVC + AFC). If ATC>AR at the profit-maximising output where MR=MC, the firm will make **subnormal** profits in the short run. (Note: It is assumed to be earning supernormal profits initially and therefore with retained earnings to invest in R&D). For example, if ATC increases from ATC0 to ATC1, the firm will make a subnormal profit equivalent to the shaded area in the diagram.

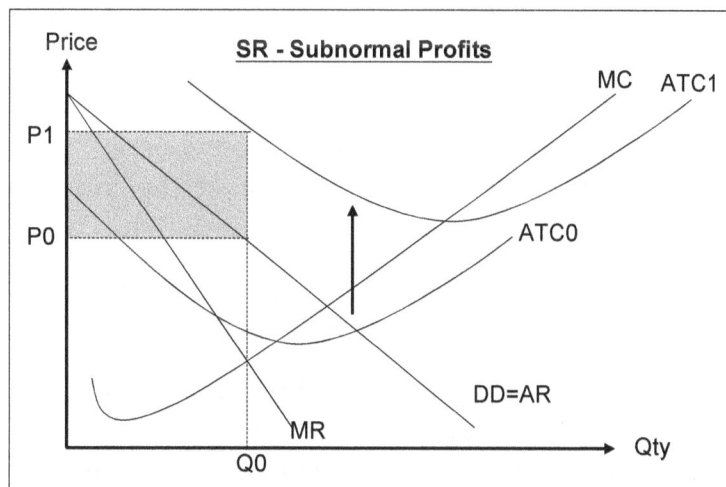

However, in the **long run**, technological advancement can enable the firm to enjoy a lower per unit COP, and allow the firm to produce the same amount of output at a lower average cost. This will cause the ATC curve of the firm to shift downwards as shown in the following diagram. This means that subsequently, the firm will be able to produce at lower marginal cost (MC) and average total cost (ATC) and make larger **supernormal** profits than initially. For example, if ATC falls from ATC0 to ATC1, the firm will make a larger supernormal profit equivalent to the shaded area in the diagram.

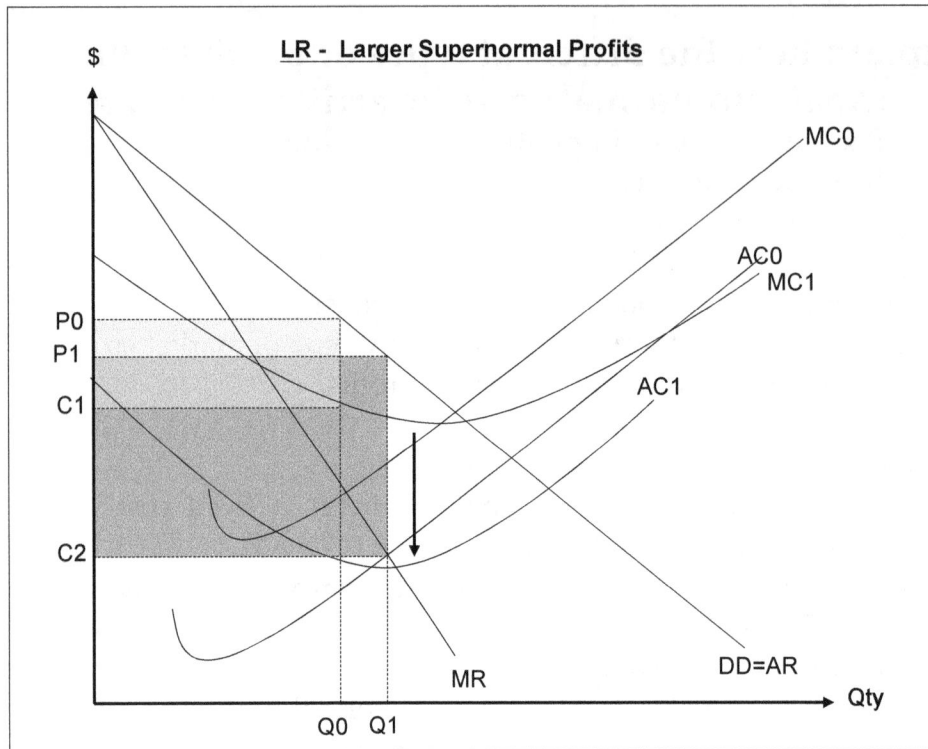

LR - Larger Supernormal Profits

$

MC0

AC0
MC1

P0
P1

C1

AC1

C2

MR

DD=AR

Qty

Q0 Q1

Evaluation:

In reality, firms must make estimates of how the technology can help to lower costs and increase profits. It has to weigh these against the initial costs of R&D and investments, as well as interest rates, which represent the opportunity cost of its investment funds.

b. Increased fixed cost

An increase in fixed costs will only increase the SRATC (SRATC = AVC + AFC). As fixed costs do not vary with output, there will be no change in MC. In the short run, an increase in fixed cost (e.g. due to advertising costs, rentals etc.) would cause the firm's SRATC curve to shift upwards, leading to a fall in profits. If ATC>AR at the profit-maximising output where MR=MC, the firm would make **subnormal** profits in the short run. (Refer to first diagram of the chapter). However, in the short run, the firm will continue to produce as long as P≥AVC.

Evaluation:

If the increase in fixed costs is due to advertising, then in the future, AR/MR can be expected to increase. The firm may be able to increase its TR due to the higher demand, and also enjoy a more price-inelastic demand. Profits would eventually increase if the increase in TR is greater than the increase in TC. For example, as illustrated in the following diagram, advertising allows the firm to experience an increase in supernormal profits from area A to area B.

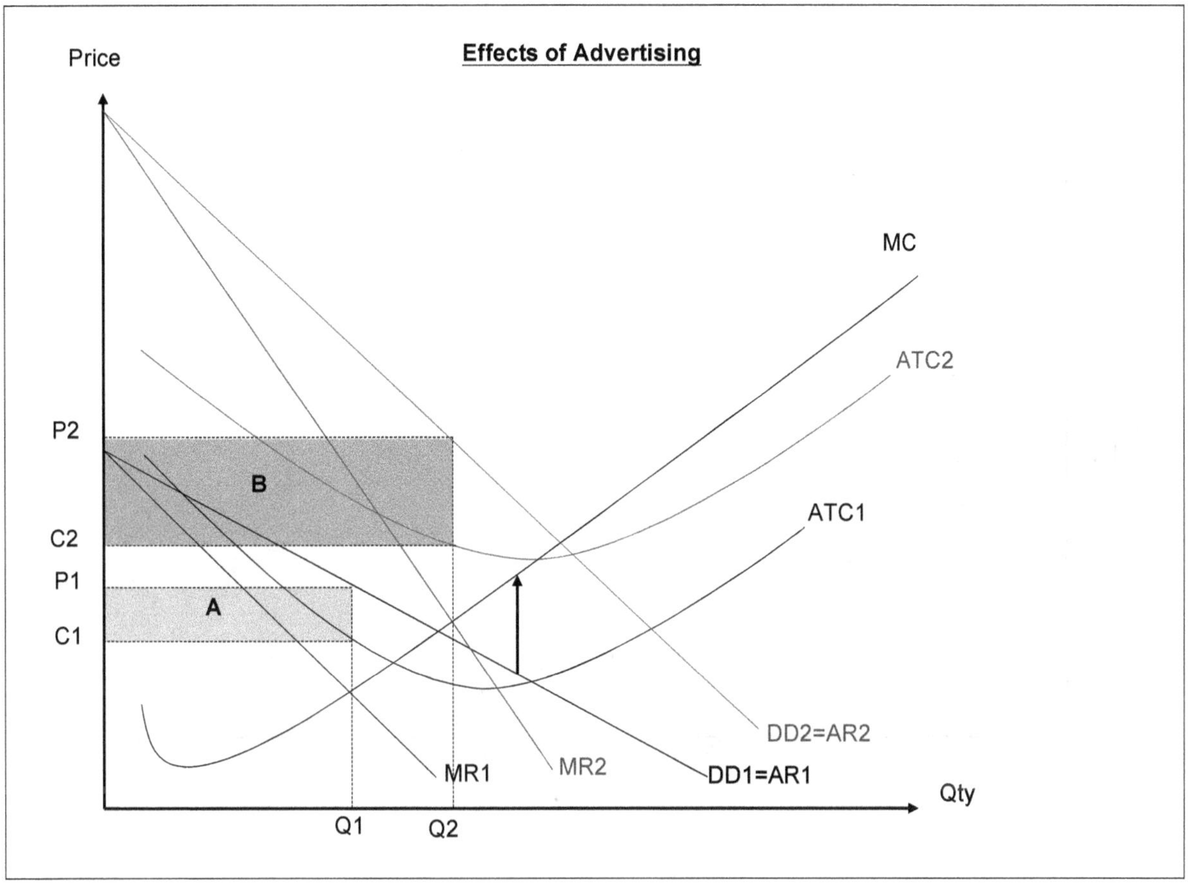

Effects of Advertising

c. Reduced demand

If demand decreases (e.g. due to new entrants in the market) the firm would experience a fall in revenue (as both price and quantity sold will decrease) and profits and may make **subnormal** profits in both the short- and long-run. If P<AVC in the SR, the firm may be forced to shut down since it cannot earn enough revenue to cover even its **variable** costs. The firm will be better off shutting down and limiting its losses to the amount of fixed costs.

The following diagram shows the firm experiencing a fall in its profits from supernormal to subnormal profits. However, in the short run, it will continue production, since P>AVC, which means its revenue earned is able to cover its variable costs, and with excess to partially pay for its fixed costs. It is better off continuing production than incurring the entire fixed cost. However if subnormal profits persist into the long run, then the firm should shut down.

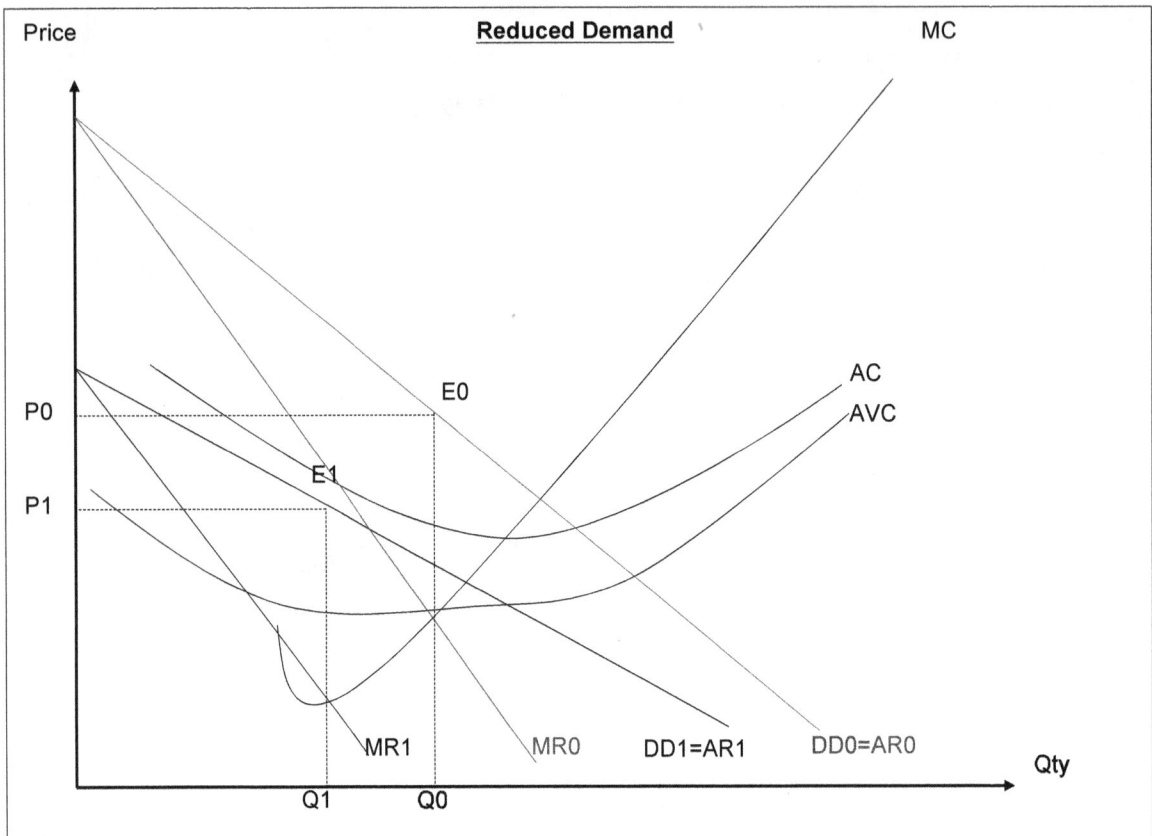

Price   **Reduced Demand**   MC

P0

P1

E0

E1

AC

AVC

MR1   MR0   DD1=AR1   DD0=AR0

Qty

Q1   Q0

41. Explain why the provision of free healthcare by the government may worsen societal welfare.

Healthcare is best defined as a **merit good** which is **deemed socially desirable by the government** but is **underconsumed if left to the free market**. Underconsumption occurs mainly due to the following three reasons:

- **Imperfect information** – Individuals may not be fully aware of the benefits of seeking early medical intervention, or engaging in preventive healthcare practices. They are less aware of the **long-term gains** of consuming healthcare services than the **short-term costs**, which must be paid in the present. Thus, Marginal Private Benefit (MPB) under imperfect information < MPB under perfect information, and underconsumption occurs.

- **Positive Externality** – Healthcare services can generate external benefits such as increased productivity of a healthy workforce for third parties (employers, the rest of the economy etc.), and reducing the spread of contagious diseases to others. Thus, Marginal Social Benefit (MSB) > MPB and underconsumption occurs.

- **A high degree of income inequality** may prevent a significant number of lower-income households from being able to afford the healthcare, resulting in a less than socially optimal amount consumed.

In order to correct this market failure, the government can **directly provide healthcare for free** to increase consumption of healthcare. In Singapore, for example, some healthcare services are provided free-of-charge for the 'pioneer generation' due to the implementation of the Pioneer Generation Package.

As shown in the following diagram, assuming MSC = MPC, the free market equilibrium is Qp where MPC = MPB, since individuals are assumed to pursue self-interest and act to maximise their own benefits. Meanwhile, the socially optimal output is Qs, where MSB = MSC. At Qp, MSB > MSC. This means that for the last unit of healthcare consumed, the benefit to society is greater than the cost of producing it. Hence, there is underconsumption of the good and more of the good should be produced. For the amount QsQp that is not consumed, the total benefit to society (cbQpQs) is greater than the total cost to society (caQpQs). This leads to a deadweight welfare loss area abc (represented by the shaded area A), which represents the welfare which society did not get to enjoy as a result of the under-consumption.

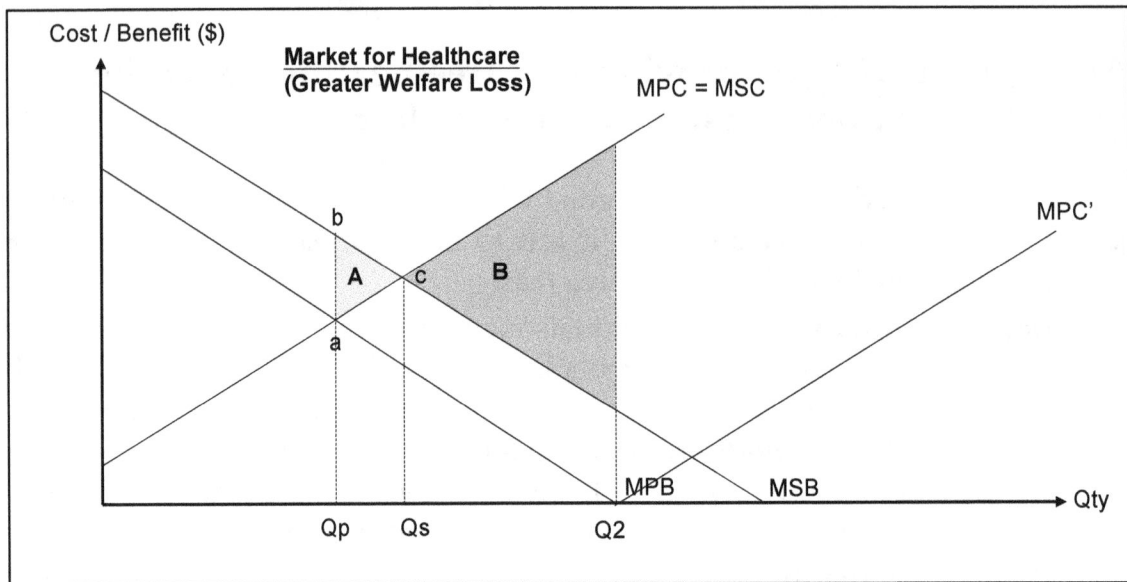

Cost / Benefit ($)

**Market for Healthcare
(Greater Welfare Loss)**

MPC = MSC

MPC'

b

A   c   B

a

MPB   MSB

Qty

Qp   Qs   Q2

However, it is possible for this to lead to **overconsumption** of healthcare, possibly leading to a greater welfare loss as compared to before government intervention. If healthcare is free, then MPC to consumers is 0 and the new free market equilibrium occurs at the point where MPB = MPC = 0. This may be depicted by a fall in the MPC curve to MPC' (reflecting a full subsidy provided at Q2). This corrects the original underconsumption of healthcare, but leads to overconsumption of healthcare and a new deadweight welfare loss equivalent to area B.

Evaluation:

Impact on Societal Welfare

Depending on the relative sizes of areas A and B, provision of healthcare by the government may or may not lead to a greater welfare loss and worsen allocative efficiency. If area A > area B, direct provision does not worsen societal welfare. There is some decrease in DWL as the amount consumed increases and is now closer to the socially optimal output. However, if area B > area A, this is a case of government failure, which occurs when societal welfare is reduced as a result of government's intervention. In such instances, the government should consider alternative means such as **subsidies** to correct the market failure, rather than providing the good for free.

Strain on Government Budget and Opportunity Cost

Apart from the deadweight loss B, the provision of free healthcare will also pose a strain on the government budget and incur significant **opportunity cost**. In this instance, the opportunity cost could be the gain in societal welfare from the provision of other merit goods such as education, which now may be foregone as funds and resources have been spent providing free healthcare instead.

In order to finance the free healthcare, the government may have to raise taxes. This can distort the incentive to work and invest, leading to adverse macroeconomic consequences.

42. Explain how a ban on a demerit good can lead to greater welfare loss.

A **demerit good** is **deemed socially undesirable by the government** and is **overconsumed** if left to the free market. This is due to two possible reasons: a) Consumers overestimate the private benefits or underestimate the private costs of consuming a demerit good due to **imperfect information**, b) it generates significant **negative externalities** which are not taken into account in the free market. Examples include **cigarettes, junk food** and **recreational drugs.**

In order to correct this market failure, the government can impose a **complete ban** on demerit goods. This is a form of **legislation**, in which the government passes laws to control business activities and prohibit/regulate behaviour.

However, it is possible for this to lead to **underconsumption** of the demerit good, possibly leading to a greater welfare loss as compared to before government intervention. As shown in the diagram below, assuming MSB = MPB, the free market equilibrium is Qp where MPC = MPB, while the socially optimal output is Qs where MSC = MSB. Due to the MEC, MSC > MPC.

If the good is banned completely, the quantity of the good consumed will fall to zero. For the amount of underconsumption, Qs, the total benefit to society that could have been obtained is equivalent to bcQs0, and the total cost to society is represented by acQs0. This leads to a deadweight welfare loss (represented by shaded area B, which represents the welfare society did not get to enjoy as a result of the under-consumption.

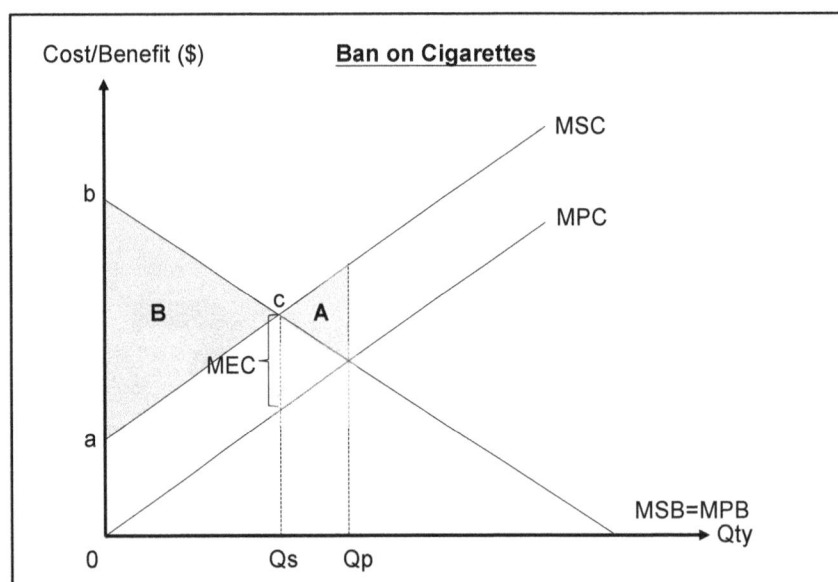

Evaluation:

Depending on the relative sizes of areas A and B, a ban may or may not lead to a greater welfare loss and Government failure. This is very much dependent on the size of the MEC. If the MEC is very large, area A is likely to be bigger than area B, and a ban does not worsen societal welfare. However, if the MEC is relatively small such that area B > area A, the government should consider alternative means such as **taxes** to correct the market failure, rather than banning the good completely.

For example, the consumption of chewing gum in Singapore is banned. This is because the negative externalities (MEC) generated by chewing gum (e.g. the external costs arising from cleanups, MRT breakdowns etc.) are assessed to be very large relative to the MPB.

43. Explain alternative objectives of a firm.

Most firms are assumed to be **profit-maximising**, which means that they aim to **increase total revenue (TR)** and **reduce total cost (TC)** in order to make the highest total profit (TR-TC).

However, firms may also aim to achieve **growth maximisation, revenue maximisation** and/or **profit satisficing**.

Growth maximisation
Firms may aim for growth through organic expansion or merger to maximise the growth in output over time. Higher growth means a higher salary, higher status and more power for the firm's managers. It also leads to greater security for the firm as there is lower takeover risk. Growth can be achieved by increasing the firm's sales volume and scale of production.

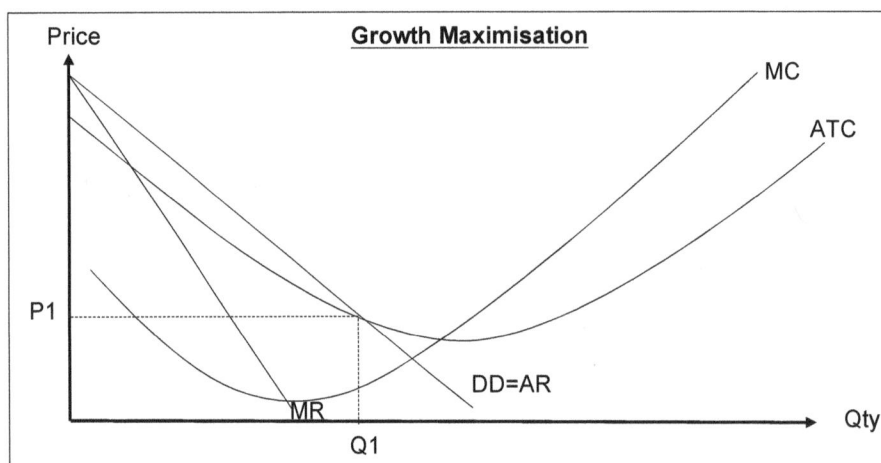

To maximise growth, the firm will produce at output Q1. This is the maximum level of output the firm can produce while still maintaining a normal profit, because P = AC. Beyond Q1, the firm would make losses. The firm's intention may also be to capture a larger **market share**, and once it has successfully done so by squeezing out competitors, it can choose to maximise profits again. Thus, while this might not seem to be profit-maximising in the short run, it is often carried out with the intent of maximising profits in the long run.

Revenue maximisation
Managers may also aim to maximise the firm's total revenue, as their salaries or wages may be directly dependent on this. For example, sales commissions are often paid as a percentage of revenue.

The condition for revenue maximisation is MR = 0, as the firm will continue to earn more revenue up to the point where the MR from selling an additional unit is 0. This means that the firm produces up to output Q1 as shown in the following diagram.

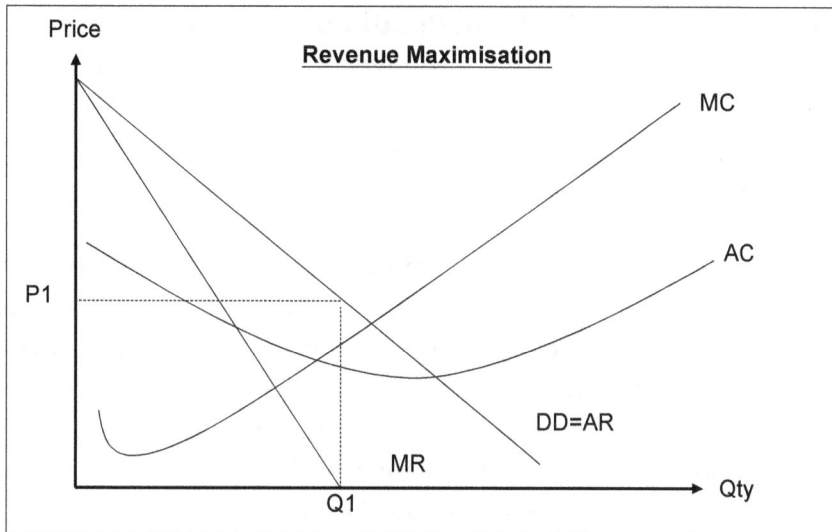

Profit Satisficing

The **principal-agent problem** may arise, as ownership and management of the firm may be separate, leading to a conflict of interests. The **owners (shareholders)** of the firm are largely concerned with maintaining profits in the short- and long-term. In the short-term, they wish to receive a decent dividend from their investment. However, in the long term, they wish to maximise the long-term value of the company which will give them a good return on their share ownership.

On the other hand, the **managers** of the firm have more experience in the day-to-day running of the firm. They are more likely to maximise their own utility, which means they are motivated by self-interest to pursue higher salaries, job status and security, power, professional excellence and so on. As the firm is a complex organization composed of many competing groups, firms may sometimes have to resort to **profit-satisficing** to resolve conflicts. This means that firms **settle for a satisfactory level of profit which is below the maximum profit,** rather than attempting to achieve the highest level of profit. For example, a manager may not sack an unproductive worker for fear of suffering a personal attack, but delivers a satisfactory level of profits to keep the shareholders happy.

44. Explain Natural Monopoly.

A natural monopoly arises when there is scope for **internal economies of scale** to be exploited over a very large range of output relative to the entire market demand. Thus, they usually exist in industries where there are large indivisible factors (large equipment or infrastructure) and **a high ratio of fixed to variable costs**. This results in average costs (AC) falling significantly over a very large range of output, as shown in the diagram below. Since the fall in AFC is more significant than the increase in AVC, ATC will continue to decline as fixed costs are spread over higher levels of output.

Therefore, in the case of a natural monopoly, one firm can usually cater to the entire market at a lower AC than two or more firms. This is because of extensive **internal economies of scale** to be reaped, and also the avoidance of **wasteful duplication of resources**. A **sole producer** that operates on a larger scale would be able to enjoy the greatest cost advantages catering to the entire market, whereas if the market was shared between 2 smaller firms, these firms will be operating on a smaller scale and incur a higher average cost of production. For example, as shown in the following diagram, the SRAC and MC of the sole producer (represented by $SRAC_{1\ Firm}$ and $MC_{1\ Firm}$ respectively) would be lower than that of firms in a split market (represented by $SRAC_{2\ Firms}$ and $MC_{2\ Firms}$ respectively). Thus, it is more efficient for a single firm to produce in this market.

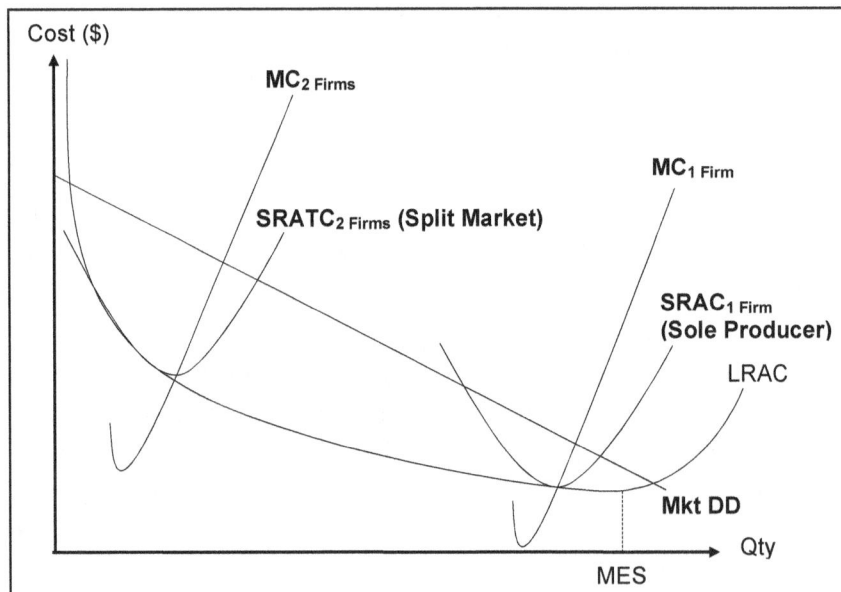

Examples of natural monopolies include **utilities** such as tap water and gas supply, as well as **local postal services.** The provision of tap water, for instance, requires high fixed costs as it involves building a national network of water pipes. Thus, having just one firm to supply water will mean that this firm can enjoy the lowest AC as high fixed costs can be spread over a greater amount of output.

Evaluation:

Government regulation
In the case of a natural monopoly, the government is likely to allow its existence rather than introducing more competitors into the market. This is because the natural monopoly can potentially benefit society through higher output and lower prices since it is able to exploit significant iEOS.

However, the government may choose to intervene to prevent the monopolist from exploiting consumers through pricing policies, such as **MC/AC Pricing Policy**. This means that the firm is forced to price its product where DD = AR = MC (represented by P3 and Q3 in the following diagram) or where DD = AR = AC (represented by P2 and Q2 on the following diagram), instead of at the profit maximising equilibrium where MR = MC.

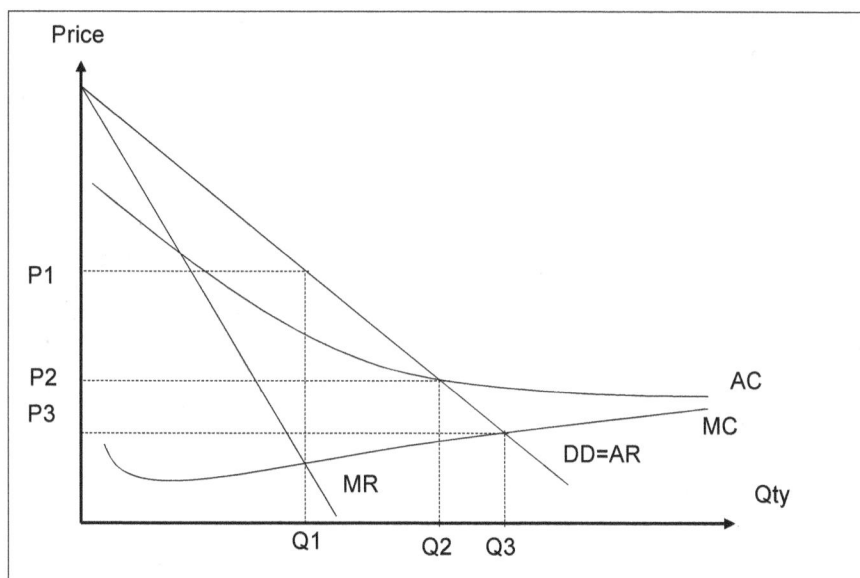

45. Explain the problems arising from Market dominance

Market Failure (Allocative Inefficiency)

Perfectly competitive (PC) firms always produce at P = MC, which is the necessary condition for achieving **allocative efficiency**. It means that society's valuation of the last unit of the good produced is equivalent to the opportunity cost of producing that unit. However, all firms with some degree of market power will produce at a point where P > MC, at their profit-maximising output where MR = MC. This is due to their **downward-sloping demand curve** and their corresponding downward-sloping MR curve.

In the PC market, the total market output is Qs where MC, which is also the supply curve of the PC market, intersects with market demand. Assuming this market is now monopolised, the monopolist produces at Q1 at its profit-maximising output where MR = MC. Thus, as compared to the PC market, it can be seen that there is **underproduction** of the good relative to the socially optimal output Qs, representing a **misallocation** of resources as less resources are allocated to the production of the good than is socially optimal. For each unit of the good underproduced (Q1-Qs), society's valuation of the good (represented by **Price** on the DD curve) is greater than the marginal cost of producing that unit (represented by **MC**). Thus, more of the good should be produced. There is a deadweight welfare loss equivalent to the shaded area as societal welfare would have increased by the deadweight loss area if more of the good had been produced.

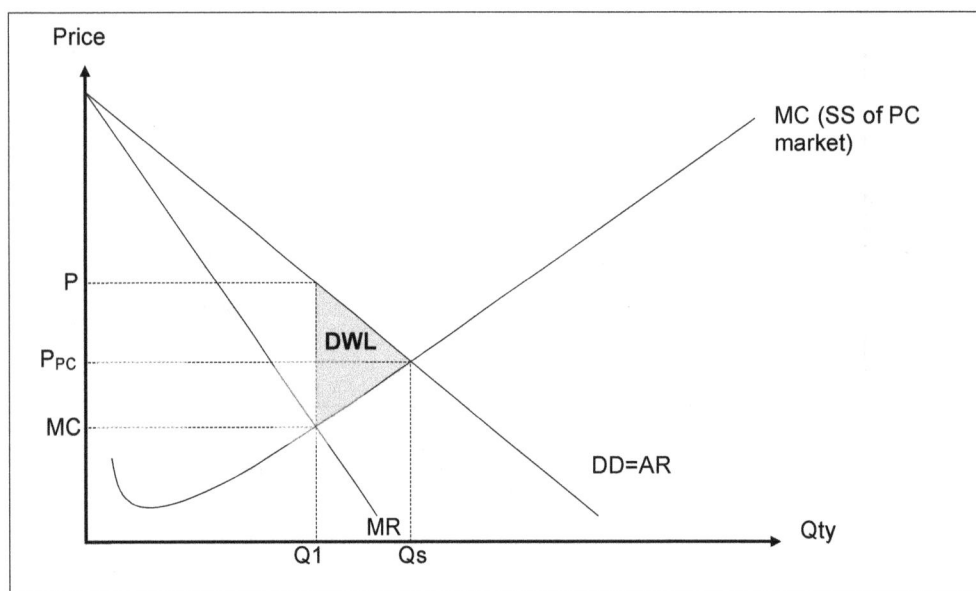

Thus, market dominance can lead to market failure as allocative efficiency cannot be achieved, even in the absence of third party costs and externalities.

Productive Inefficiency

Market dominance may also encourage greater productive inefficiency. Firms in industries with high barriers to entry can afford to be **X-inefficient and produce at a point above the ATC** curve. Such firms can afford to be complacent as they are able to retain supernormal profits in the long run (see Question 38). This is in addition to the fact that these firms are already not productively efficient from societal viewpoint, as they do not produce at min ATC, given their downward sloping demand curves.

Inequity

In addition, market dominance may worsen inequity. High barriers to entry may allow a few dominant firms to accumulate huge supernormal profits, while consumers are often exploited and have to pay higher prices for limited quantities of the good. Compared to a PC market, consumer surplus is reduced and some is transferred to the producer, increasing producer surplus. This means that high incomes are concentrated in the hands of the owners of a few dominant firms, thus increasing income inequality. Furthermore, firms with some degree of market dominance are often able to engage in **price discrimination**, which may allow producers to further capture consumer surplus. For example, in first-degree price discrimination, a firm charges a different price for each of its units sold, which corresponds to the maximum price which each consumer is willing and able to pay for each unit. As a result, the firm is able to charge prices ranging from P1 to P7 (as shown in the following diagram). This allows the producer to capture the entire consumer surplus (represented by the shaded triangle in the diagram).

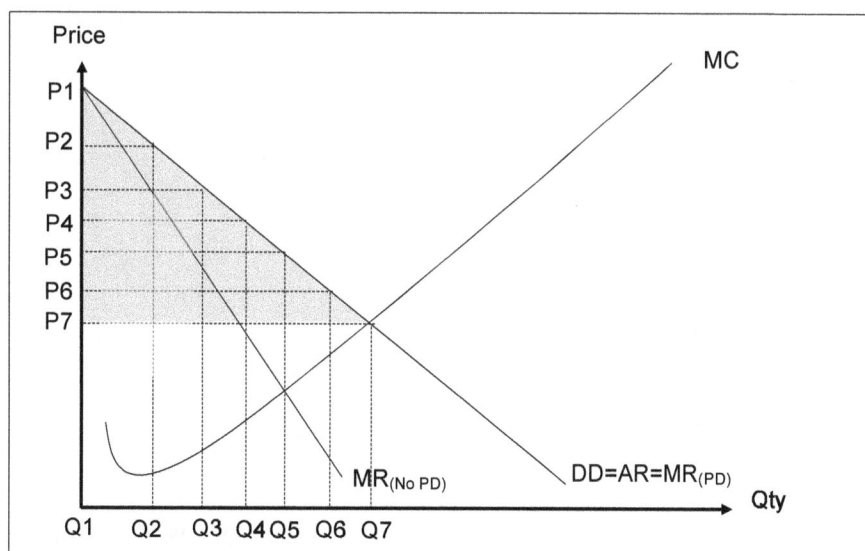

As some consumers pay even higher prices than the profit maximising price of P5, more consumer surplus and income is transferred from the consumers to the high income-earning firm owners, exacerbating income inequality.

Evaluation:

Degree of Market Dominance
The degree of market dominance enjoyed by a firm is dependent on the **barriers to entry** in that particular industry. In general, the higher the barriers to entry, the fewer the potential entrants to the market and the **lower the contestability** of the industry. This in turn allows the firm to maintain huge supernormal profits in the long run. In addition, as fewer substitutes are available, the DD = AR curve and the MR curve are more **price-inelastic.** The more dominant the firm, the greater the divergence between P and MC and the greater the deadweight loss to society, as well as the degree of allocative inefficiency.

Consumer Welfare and Equity
However, it is possible that consumer surplus and equity may not decrease, but rather increase in industries where firms enjoy market dominance. For example, in some monopolies and oligopolies, consumers may benefit from a **lower price** and a **larger output** than in a PC market. This may be attributed to the ability of the firms to **reap significant internal economies of scale**, such as in the case of a **natural monopoly**.

In addition, dominant firms earning supernormal profits have the ability to engage in **product innovation and R&D**, which can significantly improve the quality of its existing products and enhance consumer welfare. This also increases the firm's **dynamic efficiency.**

46. Explain the problems arising from income inequality.

Income inequality is defined as the unequal distribution of income and wealth. Under the free market system, goods and services are allocated to buyers according to their **dollar votes**, which reflects their willingness and ability to pay for the good. Thus, resources tend to be allocated according to income distribution. As a result, excessive income inequality can lead to **market failure**, a **fall in the material and non-material standard of living**, and other **negative macroeconomic consequences**.

Market Failure

Excessive income inequality can lead to the failure of the market to allocate resources **appropriately and equitably**. This means that even if resources are allocated efficiently, societal welfare may not be maximized. The free market only considers effective demand, which means that the lower-income who lack the ability to pay will not receive the goods and services, even though they are basic human needs and merit goods such as healthcare and education. Since the free market looks at ability to pay rather than consumer needs, a **socially desirable** level of consumption is not achieved.

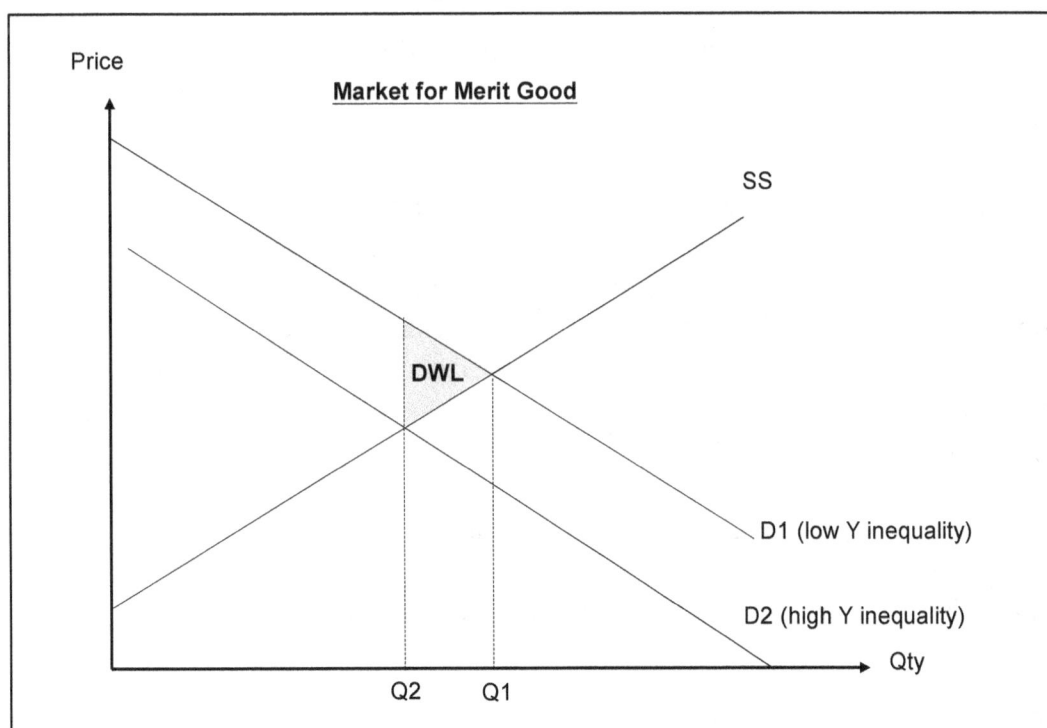

Under low income inequality, demand is D1 whereas under excessive income inequality, demand is D2, which is lower as many lower-income groups lack the ability to pay. Thus, when there is a high degree of income inequality, the free market equilibrium output of Q2 is less than the socially desirable output level of Q1. This implies that there are a significant number of lower-income earners who may need the goods but are unable to obtain them.

In summary, excessive income inequality leads to the **underallocation** of resources to **basic necessities** and **merit goods**, since the poor may be willing but unable to pay for these goods, while there is an **overallocation** of resources to luxury goods since the rich are holding on to most of the dollar votes. This is considered an inappropriate allocation of resources and is a form of market failure.

Macro Link:

Negative Macroeconomic Consequences
The poor usually have a **higher marginal propensity to consume (MPC)** and a **lower marginal propensity to save (MPS)** than the rich. This is because the rich tend to already have fulfilled their basic needs and will spend less of the additional income they receive since they already possess an abundance of goods and services. Thus as the degree of income inequality increases, the economy will experience a lower overall MPC and a higher overall MPS, leading to a lower **multiplier (k) value**. This limits the effectiveness of demand-management policies, both contractionary and expansionary, and further hinders economic growth.

Lower Material and Non-Material Standard of Living
Income inequality can also lead to a **lower material and non-material standard of living.**

Material standard of living can be compromised with high income inequality. Even with economic growth, the poor may not benefit as their real incomes may stagnate or even fall. This occurs because most of the additional income from economic growth tends to be earned by the rich in an economy with high income inequality. Hence, the poor continue to experience **low purchasing power**, hindering their ability to consume goods and services and preventing them from improving their material standard of living.

In addition, **non-material standard of living** may fall as high income inequality is often associated with political and social instability, increased stress, higher crime rates and higher levels of unrest. This in turn discourages investments and hampers economic growth, further lowering material standard of living.

Evaluation:

Inequity VS Inequality
We do not aim to achieve an **equal** income distribution, as this would not be **equitable** either. For example, those who have better skills and who are more productive should be able to earn a higher income. If not, the incentive to be more productive would be missing, which is detrimental to the economy.

Achieving a more equitable income distribution

Although the free market fails due to income inequality and government intervention such as direct provision may be required to ensure that lower income groups are able to receive merit goods and necessities, the ideal approach would be to achieve a more equitable income distribution in the first place, for example through training and education opportunities so that lower income households will be able to earn a higher income and afford more goods and services

More on the causes of income inequality and policies will be addressed in another book in this series, Ace Your Macroeconomics.

47. Explain the marginalist principle used by rational decision makers.

A rational economics agent will make a decision by **weighing the costs and benefits of any activity**, and making the choice which **maximizes utility,** i.e. **it yields the greatest benefit relative to cost.**

Due to the problem of **scarcity**, economic agents such as consumers and producers have to make **rational decisions** using marginal benefit analysis. As wants are unlimited but resources limited, there is a need to make optimal decisions in order to maximize net benefit with the scarce resources available.

Most economic decisions are made at the margin, which is the point at which the economic agent decides to take another step, such as whether to purchase another unit of the good or to produce one more unit of a particular good. In order to make their decision, they must consider **marginal benefit (MB)** and **marginal cost (MC)**, which are the benefits and costs of doing a little more of each activity. Notice that sunk costs (i.e. costs which have already been incurred and cannot be recovered) will not be considered: For example, the sunk costs of a chicken rice hawker stall (such as renovation costs) will be considered a part of the AC and not the MC, and thus will not be taken into account in deciding how much output to produce.

Consumers
Consumers will spend on a particular item until the benefit gained from spending one more dollar on the good is less than the benefit that can be gained from spending that dollar on another item. Referring to the following diagram, consumers will consume until Q0 where **MPB = MPC,** or Marginal Private Benefit = Marginal Private Cost of consuming that particular good. If MPB > MPC (e.g. at Q1), the consumer will benefit from consuming more of the good. However, if MPC > MPB (e.g. at Q2), overconsumption will occur and the consumer's income could be better spent on other goods from which he/she will derive greater benefit.

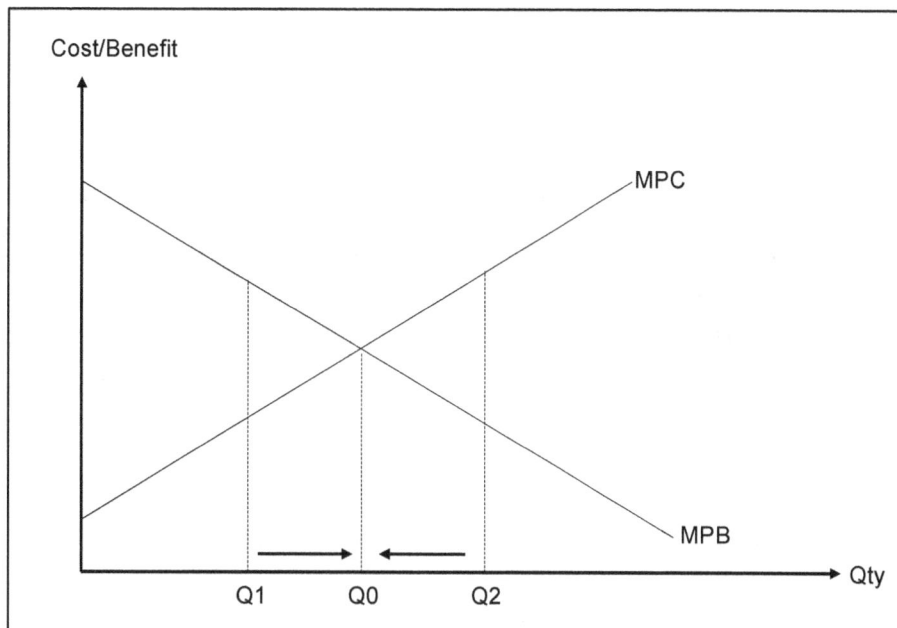

Producers

Producers use the marginalist principle to decide on the level of production. The profit-maximising output for firms is **MR = MC, where MC is increasing**.

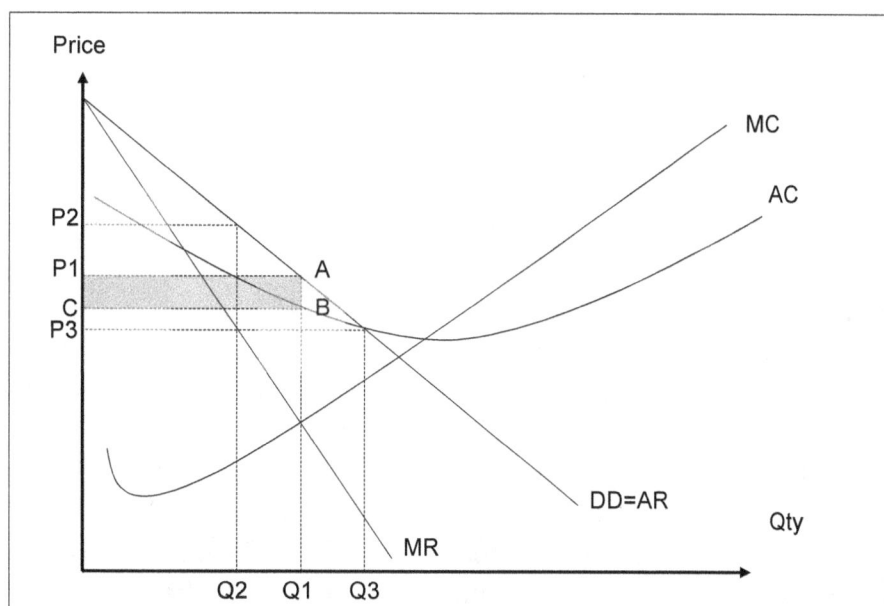

With reference to the diagram above, at Q2 where MR > MC, the additional TR earned from the last unit of output sold is greater than the additional cost incurred from its production. Thus, the firm can increase its total profits if it increases production. **Profits are not maximized when MR > MC.**

At Q3, however, since MR < MC, this means that the sale of the last unit of output adds less to TR than the additional cost incurred from its production. Thus, the last unit of output produced will result in a fall in total profits. The firm can increase its total profits if it decreases its level of production, and **profits are not maximized**

105

when MR < MC.

Hence, at Q1 where MR = MC and at P1, the firm is able to maximise profits and its total profits are measured as the area P1ABC.

Producers can also use marginal analysis to decide how many units of a particular resource they should allocate to production. For example, they hire labour until hiring one more worker adds **the same amount** to sales revenue than his or her wage, that is, up to the point where Marginal Revenue Product (**MRP**) = Marginal Resource Cost (**MRC**).

Government
The government can also use the marginalist principle to determine the socially optimal amount of output in order to implement policies to correct market failure or to decide which public goods it should produce (and in what quantity). The socially optimal output is where Marginal Social Benefit (**MSB**) = Marginal Social Cost (**MSC**). When MSB > MSC, society would benefit from greater allocation of resources to the production and consumption of the good; when MSB < MSC, society would be better off if fewer resources were devoted to the production and consumption of the good.

Evaluation:

Note that the marginalist principle is **not** used when the firm makes a decision to shut down or remain in business (in the long and short run). In such an instance, the firm would be making decisions based on Average Variable Cost (AVC) and Average Total Cost (ATC) versus Average Revenue (AR). In the long run, the firm will only remain in business as long as AR > ATC, as it must be able to earn at least as much revenue as the costs it incurs in order to break even. In the short run, however, the firm will be willing to remain in business as long as AR ≥ AVC. This means that the firm is at least earning enough to cover the variable costs, and if AR > AVC, the revenue earned by the firm will also partially cover its fixed costs. The firm will thus continue to produce in the short run, as it will suffer a smaller loss than if it shuts down and incurs the total amount of fixed costs. There would also be some hope that DD/AR may increase in the future, allowing the firm to be more profitable in the long run.

48. What is Market failure and Government failure?

Market failure is the failure of the market to allocate resources **efficiently** or **equitably**. More specifically, it is defined as the failure of the market to achieve **allocative efficiency**, which means that resources are not allocated in a manner that maximises societal welfare. It leads to over-allocation or under-allocation of resources relative to the socially optimal level ($P \neq MC$ or $MSB \neq MSC$), or the failure of the market to achieve a socially **appropriate allocation of resources** due to excessive income inequality.

Government failure occurs when government intervention reduces societal welfare, resulting in a more inefficient allocation of resources as compared to when there was no government intervention.

Evaluation:

Reasons for market failure
Reasons for market failure include:
- Externalities/third party costs and benefits are not taken into account
- Non-provision of public goods
- Under or overconsumption of merit and demerit goods
- Market imperfections
    - Market dominance
    - Imperfect information
    - Immobility of factors of production

Reasons for government failure
- Productive inefficiencies and poor quality due to lack of profit motive
- Imperfect information (e.g. Lack of technical information about externalities, poor information on market conditions)
- Failure to take into account of the opportunity costs incurred in utilizing Government resources
- Policies may worsen inequity despite reducing allocative inefficiency. For example, if a tax is imposed to address demerit goods, it helps to reduce allocative inefficiency by causing producers to internalise the negative exernality, causing the MPC to increase such that it coincides with, or is at least closer to the MSC. While this helps to reduce allocative inefficiency, indirect taxes tend to be **regressive** in nature, which means that they often take up a **larger proportion** of the poor's income. As a result, they tend to worsen income inequality in the process.

49. Explain 2 types of externalities and their implications.

An externality arises when the wellbeing of a **third party**, which is not directly involved in the production/consumption of the good, **incurs costs** or **receives benefits** from the production/consumption of the good, yet **does not receive nor pay any compensation** for this effect. Externalities may be **negative** or **positive** in nature.

Negative Externality
Negative externalities refer to **external costs** incurred by third parties from the production/consumption of the good, yet they are not compensated for these external costs. Common examples include cigarettes, traffic congestion (usually from **consumption**) and pollution (usually from **production**).

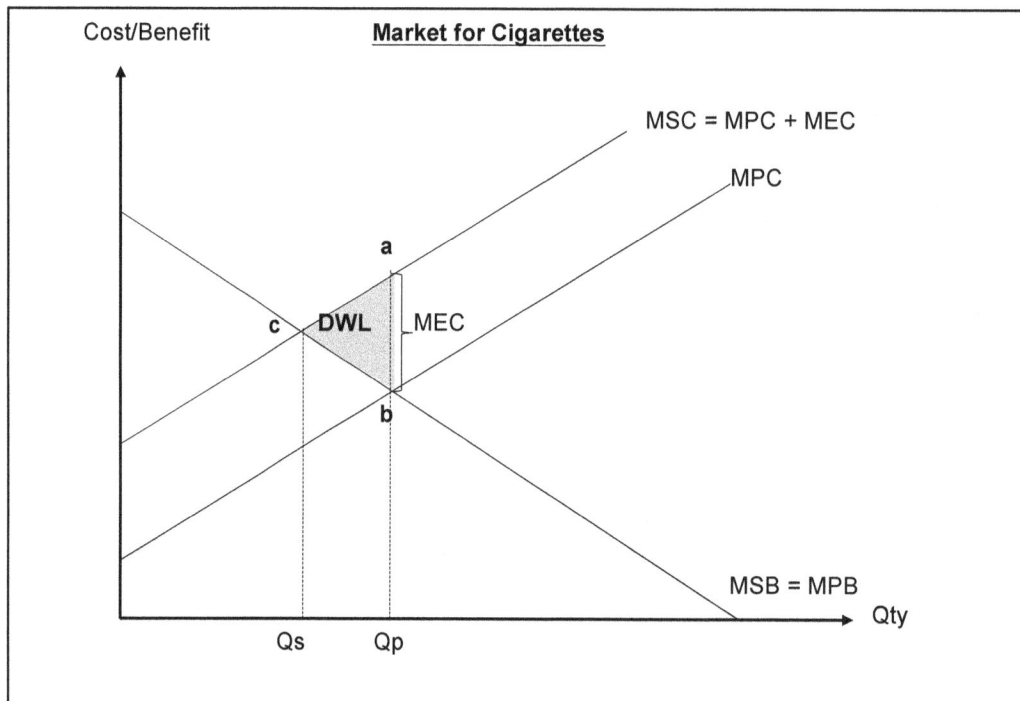

- For example, consider the negative externality from **smoking**. Smokers may take into account the private costs of smoking such as the cost of each packet of cigarettes, but fail to consider the negative impact of second-hand smoke on surrounding individuals or family members. This toxic 'passive smoking' can lead to increased healthcare costs to the third parties, but are not considered by the individual smoker.

- These external costs (known as the marginal external cost (**MEC**)) lead to a **divergence** between the marginal private cost (**MPC**) and the marginal social cost (**MSC**), in which **MSC = MPC+MEC**.

- Assuming that **marginal private benefit (MPB) = marginal social benefit (MSB)**, the free market equilibrium is Qp where **MPC = MPB**, assuming that individual consumers and producers are self-seeking and aim only to maximise their own utility.

- However, the socially optimal output is Qs where MSC = MSB, which means that the opportunity cost to society of the last unit of cigarettes consumed is equal to the benefit to society of consuming the good. An efficient allocation of resources would be achieved.

- Thus, the market has failed to achieve allocative efficiency, as there is overconsumption of cigarettes and overallocation of resources to the production of cigarettes.

- For each unit overconsumed, society would have been better off if resources had been diverted to the provision of other goods and services from which greater benefits could have been derived. For the amount of overconsumption QpQs, the cost to society **acQsQp** exceeds the benefits to society **bcQsQp**. This leads to a deadweight welfare loss equivalent to **abc**.

Positive Externality

Positive externalities are **external benefits** received by third parties for the production/consumption of the good, yet they do not have to pay for these benefits. Examples include the benefits from R&D (usually from **production**), education and vaccination/immunisation programmes (from **consumption**).

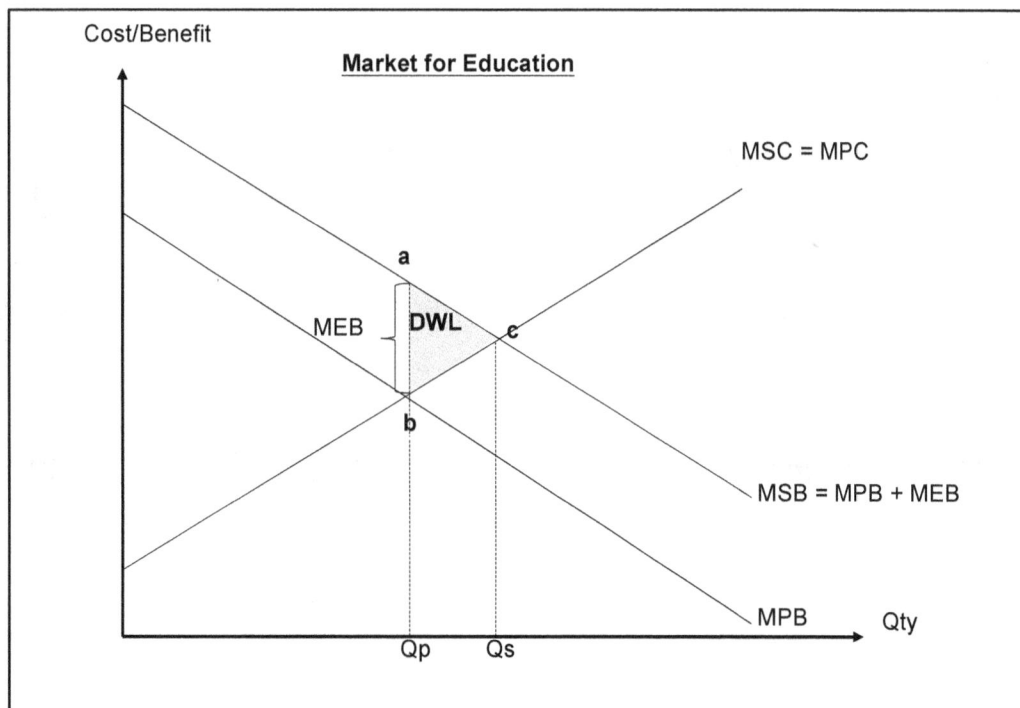

- For example, consider the positive externality from consuming **education**. While the private benefits of education include higher potential wage and job security, the external benefits to third parties (such as firms) include a more productive workforce and a more civil and educated populace which could benefit the society in general, in terms of lower crime rates and greater social stability.

- These external benefits lead to a **divergence** between the marginal private benefit (**MPB**) and the marginal social benefit (**MSB**) in which **MSB = MPB + MEB**

- Assuming that marginal private cost (**MPC**) = marginal social cost (**MSC**), the free market equilibrium is Qp where MPC = MPB, assuming that individual consumers and producers are self-seeking and aim only to maximise their own utility.

- However, the socially optimal output is Qs where MSC = MSB, which means that the cost to society of the last unit of education produced is equal to the societal benefit of consuming that unit of education. An efficient allocation of resources would be achieved.

- Thus, the free market has failed to achieve allocative efficiency and there is underallocation of resources to the production and consumption of education.

- For the amount of underconsumption QpQs, the benefits to society **acQsQp** exceed the cost to society **bcQsQp**. This leads to a deadweight welfare loss equivalent to **abc**.

Tip

Identifying the Deadweight Loss Area
The deadweight loss area always points towards the socially optimal output level, Qs.
It is also bounded by:

- Equilibrium quantity in free market, and the socially optimal quantity (Qp and Qs)
- MSB and MSC

---

50. Explain 3rd degree price discrimination.

Price discrimination is the practice of selling the same product to different consumers at different prices, where the difference in price charged is not due to differences in cost.

In **third degree price discrimination**, a firm sells the same product at different prices to different groups of consumers, for reasons not due to cost differences. In order for third degree price discrimination to be **possible and profitable**, the following conditions must be met:

1. The seller must be able to segment the market into **different, identifiable submarkets** that can be kept **separate**, each with a **different PED**. Furthermore, there must be **no possibility of resale** between the different two markets, to prevent **arbitrage** from occurring. Arbitrage occurs when the same good is bought in the cheaper market and sold in the more expensive market at a lower price, effectively restoring price equality.
2. The seller must be a **price-setter** with a significant degree of market power.

The total output must be such that $\mathbf{MR_{Total} = MC}$ (where MC is rising), otherwise the firm would be able to increase its profits by increasing or reducing its total output. In addition, the total output must be divided between the two submarkets such that the **MRs of each group are equal**. Otherwise, the firm would not be maximising profits as it could easily sell more output to the group with greater MR to increase its profits.

The relative prices to be charged in each submarket depend on their differing PED values. **A higher price is charged in the market where demand is relatively more price-inelastic while a lower price is charged in the market where demand is relatively more price-elastic.**

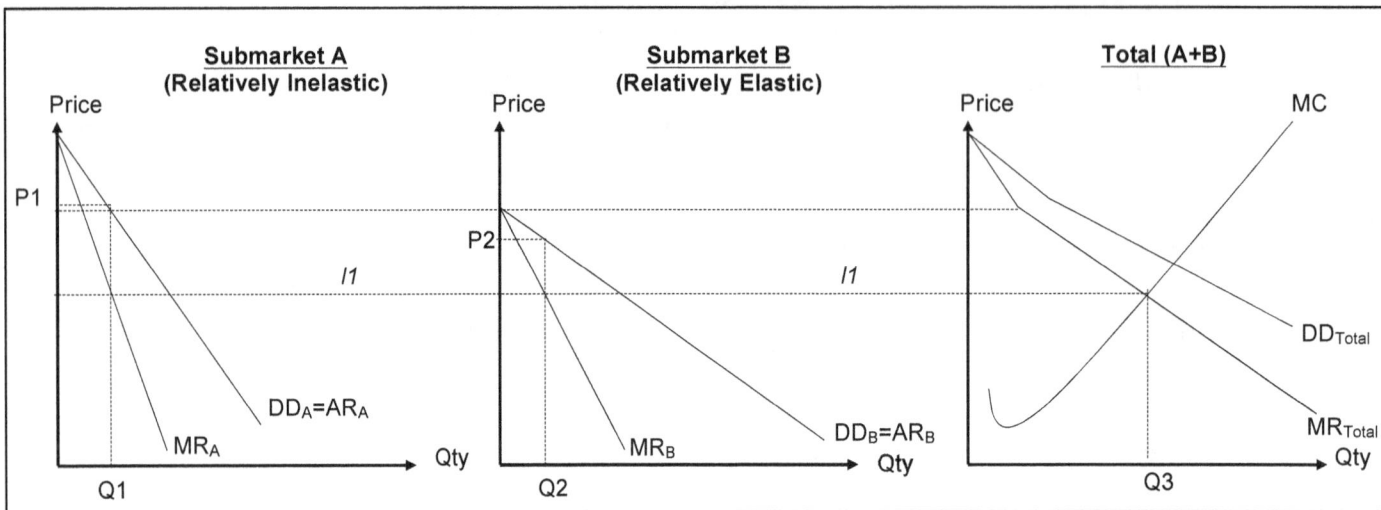

In the diagram shown, the conditions for price discrimination have been met.

- The entire market has been segmented into two different submarkets, **submarket A and B**, which we assume to be identifiable and separable.
- To maximize profit, the firm equates MR_{total} to MC. This allows it to determine its profit-maximising output, **Q3**.
- To divide output Q3 between the two submarkets, the firm now equates the MC of the total market with the MR of each individual market ($MC = MR_{Total} = MR_A = MR_B$). This is represented by the line $l1$, which is extrapolated across the MR curves of both submarkets. It is important to note that for each submarket, **MR is also equal.** If the MR were higher in submarket A, then the firm will be able to increase profits by selling more output in submarket A than submarket B. Likewise, if the MR were higher in submarket B, then the firm will be able to increase profits by selling more output in submarket B than A.
- This determines output and price level in submarket A (Q1 and P1), as well as output and price level in submarket B (Q2 and P2), where **Q3 = Q1 + Q2**
- **Higher price** (P1) is charged in submarket A where demand is more **price-inelastic**, while a **lower price** (P2) is charged in submarket B where demand is more **price-elastic**.

Note that a more concise answer may be required in exams due to time constraints, and this explanation is merely for your own understanding. The key points to include in an exam question on 3rd degree PD have been highlighted at the end of the chapter.

An example of third degree price discrimination is advanced airticket booking, as opposed to last minute airticket booking. The former is cheaper since consumers are likely to have the luxury of time to explore other alternatives (hence DD is more price-elastic), whereas the latter is likely to be more expensive as consumers are likely to be facing time constraints and buying the tickets may be a matter of urgency (DD is more price-inelastic). Note that the airticket market meets the conditions for successful price discrimination because it is possible to separate these two submarkets (early ticket bookers and last-minute bookers) based on the point of time at which they book their tickets; for example, those who book tickets within a week of the flight would be considered last-minute bookers. Furthermore, airline operators usually exist in an **oligopoly** where each individual firm possesses a significant degree of market power, enabling it to effectively exercise price discrimination.

Another example is students being offered discounted rates in cinemas. The cinema market meets the conditions for successful price discrimination as students are easily identifiable by their student passes and locally, cinemas operate within an oligopolistic market structure, allowing them to enjoy significant market power. Since the price of movie tickets take up a larger proportion of students' allowances, their demand for movie tickets tends to be more price-elastic and as such, they are typically charged less than adults for the same movie tickets.

Evaluation:

Inter-temporal Price Discrimination/Peak Load Pricing
Sometimes, people are charged higher prices at peak periods as compared to off-peak periods. Examples include plane ticket and train fares. The term 'inter-temporal price discrimination', also known as peak load pricing, may be misleading in that it is not necessarily a true form of price discrimination.

Although it can be argued that the higher price charged at peak periods could be due to the more inelastic demand during peak periods (e.g. fewer substitutes available when travellers are rushing for time or need to reach desired destinations more urgently), most of the time, the difference in prices may also be due to **differences in production cost.** For example, firms may have to operationalise additional equipment with higher operating costs, and hire more workers to meet increased demand. Due to the Law of Diminishing Marginal Returns, MC increases with output, leading to higher costs and hence prices. In such an instance, peak load pricing may be due to higher costs rather than Price Discrimination. In reality, the price differences are likely to be due to both the practice of Price Discrimination as well as cost differences.

3rd Degree Price Discrimination

CHECK: Are <u>conditions</u> for 3rd Degree PD met?
- Price-setting firm with significant market power
- Different, identifiable submarkets with different PED
- Submarkets can be kept separate, with no possibility of resale/arbitrage

IF YES
- Draw 3rd degree diagram
- Clarify what the 2 distinct submarkets are. (For simplification, we call them A and B here)
- $MR_{total} = MC$ at profit maximizing output
- $MC = MR_A = MR_B$
- Determine Price and Output level in each submarket, where $Q_{total} = Q_A + Q_B$
- More price-inelastic submarket = Higher price; more price-elastic submarket = lower price

IF NO
- Most important factor to consider: Are there different MCs for each submarket?
- Are the goods really identical?

51. Explain reasons for Privatisation and Deregulation.

Privatisation is defined as the **sale**, in whole or in part, of **public** (state-owned) **enterprises to the private sector**. Its purpose is usually to **subject the firm to market forces**, increasing the incentive to be productively efficient and to allow consumers to benefit from **higher output, better quality** products and **lower prices**. An example would be the liberalisation of the telecommunications sector in Singapore, in which the government changed Singtel's status from a statutory board to a publicly listed company in 1993.

Deregulation involves the liberalization of markets through the **removal of restrictive rules to encourage competition** in the private sector. The key objective of deregulation is to increase the **contestability** of the market, reducing allocative inefficiency and increasing consumer welfare. After privatizing the telecommunications market, the government proceeded to deregulate it further in 2000 by offering more telecommunications licenses, which led to new entrants like Starhub and M1, introducing greater competition into the sector. The Singapore government has also deregulated the banking and finance sector by offering banking licenses to foreign banks.

Increased Consumer Welfare (Price, output, quality, choice)
Increased competition leads to a **lower and more price-elastic demand** curve (from DD0 to DD1) for each incumbent firm as the number of substitutes increases. As the market moves towards a more competitive equilibrium, consumers are able to benefit from lower prices (P0 to P1) and greater output (due to the increase in market supply*) resulting in an **increase in consumer surplus** and a **reduction of the deadweight welfare loss to society** (as can be seen in the following diagram). As competition intensifies, the quality of firms' products becomes an important factor of non-price competitiveness and firms may engage in **product innovation** to create new products or improve existing products, leading to greater consumer choice (due to the increase in both the **number of firms** and the **variety of goods produced**), and better **product quality**.

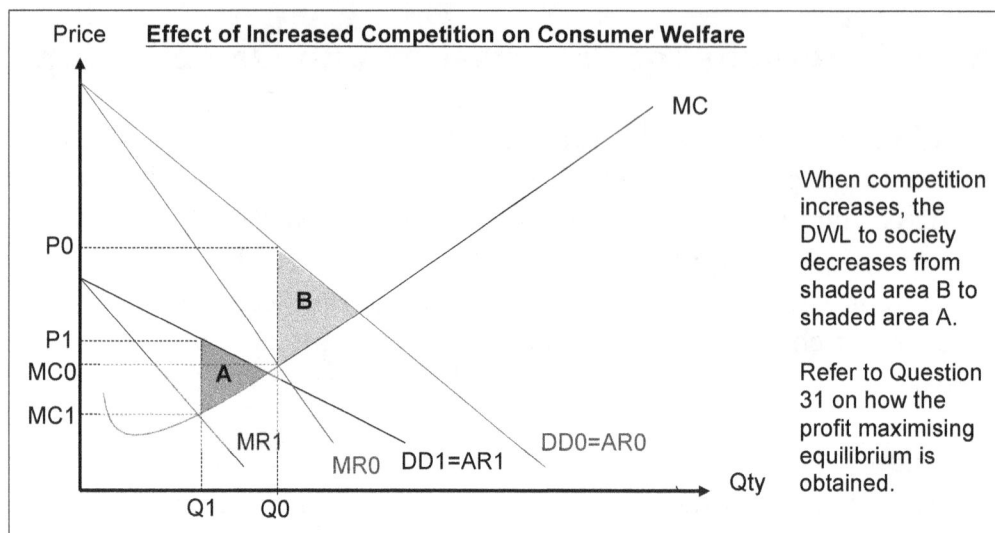

Effect of Increased Competition on Consumer Welfare

When competition increases, the DWL to society decreases from shaded area B to shaded area A.

Refer to Question 31 on how the profit maximising equilibrium is obtained.

*From the diagram shown, **firm output** decreases from Q0 to Q1 due to the increase in competition. However, the entrance of new firms into the market should result in an overall increase in **market output**.

Economic Efficiency

Allocative inefficiency is reduced as the market becomes more contestable, reducing the monopoly power of individual firms. This can be observed from the **reduction in the divergence between P and MC** (the divergence between P1 and MC1 is less than the divergence between P0 and MC0). In addition, the increase in competition incentivises **productive efficiency** as firms must strive to use the lowest cost method of production in order to translate cost savings into lower prices to match up against rivals and 'squeeze' rival firms out of the market. If not, they risk being eliminated from the market in the long term.

Benefits to Government's Budget

The sale of profitable state assets to the private sector can help to **generate revenue** and higher corporate tax receipts for the government. It can also reduce the need for the government to finance losses incurred by state enterprises.

Evaluation:

Long-term loss of revenue

In the long run, the state may lose the potential future profits from profitable state industries, thus the government may experience a net loss of revenue. However, this may be quite a remote possibility as most state-owned enterprises are notoriously inefficient and tend to suck up government resources instead. Furthermore, from the societal viewpoint, this loss may be outweighed by the gains in efficiencies and consumer welfare.

Greater Inefficiency

If privatisation results in a public-sector monopoly being replaced by a private-sector monopoly, there will be no increase in competition and consumer welfare. In fact, allocative inefficiency which arises from market dominance will be worse, since the monopolist is unlikely to act in the interest of societal welfare, and is unlikely to take positive/negative externalities, equity or achieving allocative efficiency into account.

Even if new entrants emerge, if the industry remains an oligopoly, there could be collusion, which may lead to consumers being exploited in terms of higher prices and lower output, contributing to a high degree of allocative inefficiency since a collusive oligopoly fundamentally acts like a monopoly.

In addition, the entrance of new firms into the market may lead to duplication and higher costs. This is inefficient and wasteful in cases of natural monopolies such as public utilities (water, gas etc.) and may lead to higher costs and lower consumer welfare.

Increased Market Dominance

Deregulation could potentially lead to larger, more dominant foreign firms gaining market share at the expense of local firms. Market dominance in the industry could potentially increase, offsetting the gains from increased competition.

Competition Laws

Ultimately, privatisation and deregulation should be accompanied by competition laws to ensure that competition is fair and that consumers are not exploited through excessively high prices. If the intention is to increase competition, regulators should prevent the emergence of private-sector monopolies as well as tacit collusion since this would defeat the original purpose of privatisation/deregulation.

In the context of the deregulation of the telecommunications sector in Singapore, the Infocomm Development Authority (IDA) has been actively monitoring the actions of Singtel, Starhub and M1. On the flip side, this could mean an increase in regulatory costs and an additional burden on the government's budget.

Loss of Internal Economies of Scale and Dynamic Efficiency

As more firms enter the market, the demand for existing firms' products will decrease (assuming market demand remains constant), leading to a loss of revenue and profits for existing firms. The loss of supernormal profits reduces firm's ability to engage in R&D and invest in advanced technologies, leading to a loss of dynamic efficiency and consumer welfare in the long term.

In addition, the fall in demand for existing firms' products means that firms will produce less output and operate on a smaller scale. Thus, they may enjoy fewer internal economies of scale, leading to higher average costs, which could translate to higher prices for consumers.

52. Explain reasons for Nationalisation.

Nationalisation refers to the public ownership of an entire industry, which was previously owned by the private sector, and occurs mainly in the case of **natural monopolies**. The government takes over the provision of goods and services to **prevent monopoly pricing**, especially if the goods are essential or of strategic national interest. It can also eliminate **allocative inefficiency**, reducing the problem of market failure arising from market dominance, externalities and imperfect information.

Greater Efficiency

Natural monopolies are usually allowed to exist on the basis that cost advantages due to internal economies of scale can be exploited over a very large range of output, allowing consumers to benefit from lower prices and larger output. Since it may be assumed that it is the governments responsibility to care for the social welfare of its people, nationalisation provides greater assurance that these monopolies will **work in the public interest to maximize efficiency, and protect rather than exploit consumers**. For example, in industries that generate externalities, government production will take these externalities into account to ensure that the socially optimal output is produced.

Nationalisation also helps to increase efficiency by eliminating overlapping activities of competing suppliers, **minimising wasteful duplication** by merging operations into a single, more productive and efficient state-owned monopoly. This is particularly significant in industries supplying services such as electricity, water and transportation. In Singapore, for example, the industry for water supply has been nationalised and is under the control of the Public Utilities Board (PUB).

Equity

A nationalised industry may also practice **price discrimination** to provide essential or merit goods at affordable prices for the poor. Price discrimination involves selling the same product to different groups of consumers at different prices, for reasons not due to differences in production cost. For example, in public transport, lower income groups (such as the elderly and students) may be offered lower prices as producers can compensate for the lower revenue from this group of consumers by charging working adults higher prices which they are able and willing to pay.

Nationalisation also ensures that certain goods are produced, even at **prices below the cost of production**, because they are deemed essential to the public interest. For example, postal services and railway services in the suburbs are unlikely to be profitable due to the lack of demand in these areas, and a profit-maximising monopoly would reduce services in rural areas, significantly reducing the welfare of citizens in these areas. Thus, the government takes over the production of these services in the interest of the nation, even if it makes subnormal profits in the short and long run in order to ensure greater levels of social welfare.

Stability
Nationalisation can help to **minimise the adverse impact of economic shocks,** which may destabilize the economy. For example, the failure of large firms may seriously jeopardise economic stability, particularly if the industry is a strategic one or essential to the economy. In such instances, nationalisation can help to restore economic confidence so as to attract investments to other sectors, and help to minimise the loss of jobs for the economy. A recent example is the full or part nationalisation of several UK banks in 2008 as a result of the US financial crisis.

Economic growth
Governments possess **significant funds and capital,** which may be necessary to carry out R&D in certain industries. In some cases, the government may be the only body capable of providing the **massive investments and capital expenditure required**. If the industries involved are deemed vital for economic growth, nationalisation may be a preferred option as it can help to achieve growth and stability for the economy. An example would be the nationalisation of railways in the UK in 1948 to help rebuild the network infrastructure after the destruction caused by World War II.

Evaluation:

Inefficiency
Due to the **lack of profit motive**, state-owned firms may lack the incentive to be cost-conscious and productively efficient, and tend to be **bureaucratic** and disorganized in nature as compared to private enterprises. Nationalisation may also create excessively large and overly-bureaucratic organisations which suffer from **internal diseconomies of scale**. If these firms are involved in the supply of services like electricity and transport, other industries will also be affected by the higher cost of production, lowering their competitiveness as well.

Poor Quality / Lack of Innovation
Due to political reasons, prices are usually still kept low. However, there is no guarantee that the products will be of better quality. Without the profit motive, there is little or no incentive for the nationalised firm to engage in R&D to innovate its existing products, leading to the loss of dynamic efficiency. The lack of competition poses further problems, as firms will lack incentive to innovate or improve the quality of its products.

Consumer Choice
As the nationalised firm is still a monopoly, albeit a state-owned one, consumers will still have to tolerate the limited product choices available.

Government Failure and Opportunity Cost
Even if the government does successfully take over the industry, it is possible that

other sources of **government failure** such as inefficiency and imperfect information may persist, reducing the benefits from nationalisation. In addition, nationalisation may put a strain on the government budget, especially if the industry involved is a loss-making one. A massive **opportunity cost** may be incurred as the resources might have been better employed elsewhere to improve societal welfare.

Political Reasons

Nationalisation may also be undertaken for political instead of economic reasons, such as for national pride. In such instances, it is likely to lead to greater inefficiencies, with costs outweighing potential benefits.

53. Explain how Imperfect Information leads to Market failure.

Imperfect information is a characteristic of all imperfectly competitive markets. It occurs when people have inaccurate, incomplete, uncertain or misunderstood data, causing them to make 'wrong' choices and preventing them from consuming/producing at optimal levels.

There are four types of imperfect information which can lead to market failure – Imperfect information in **merit and demerit goods**, imperfect information in **imperfect competition**, imperfect information in **persuasive advertising**, and **asymmetric information**.

Merit/Demerit Goods

In the case of demerit and merit goods, consumers **do not recognise the true costs/benefits** of consuming the good, and will **over- or underestimate** marginal private cost (**MPC**) or marginal private benefit (**MPB**).

For example, in the case of demerit goods like cigarettes, individual consumers may not be fully aware of the long-term private costs of smoking, such as lung cancer and poor health which could lead to future healthcare costs, loss of income and leisure. Conversely, smokers may only consider the short term benefits from smoking – to satisfy their addiction. Thus, the long-term costs which consumers are less aware of could lead to a divergence between DD under imperfect information and the DD under perfect information, which is lower.

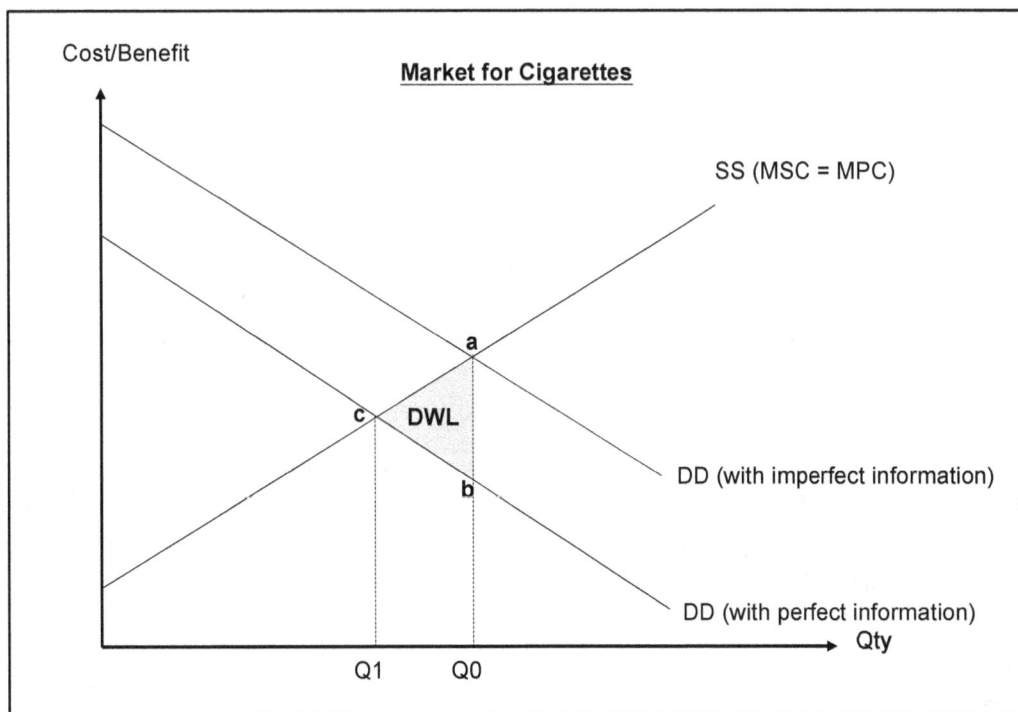

Thus, in the case of demerit goods, the good is neither produced nor consumed at the socially optimal output. Q0 of the good is consumed, yet the socally optimal output level is Q1. For each unit overconsumed, society would have been better off if resources had been diverted to the provision of other goods and services from which greater benefits could have been derived. The cost to society, acQ1Q0, exceeds the benefits to society, bcQ1Q0, by the area abc which is also the **deadweight loss to society**. This is **allocatively inefficient**, and hence there is **market failure.**

Conversely, in the case of merit goods such as healthcare, individual consumers may not be aware of the long-term gains of seeking early treatment and engaging in preventive healthcare practices. Such services may enable consumers to enjoy greater life expectancy and maintain a better overall quality of life, but consumers may underestimate these benefits while considering the short-term costs of paying for these services. As shown in the following diagram, this leads to a divergence between DD under imperfect information and the DD under perfect information, which is higher.

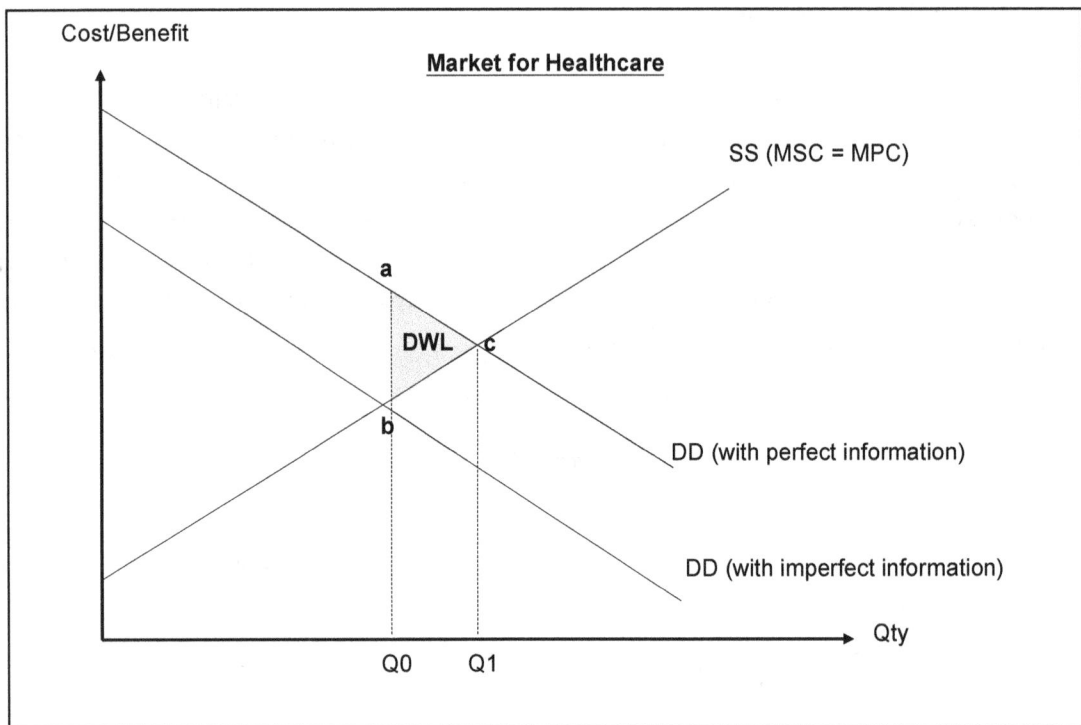

Q0 of the good is consumed, yet the socially optimal amount is Q1. For each unit underconsumed, society would have been better off if resources had been diverted to the provision of more healthcare services. The benefit to society, acQ1Q0, exceeds the cost to society, bcQ1Q0, by the area abc which is also the **deadweight loss to society**. This is **allocatively inefficient**, and hence there is **market failure.**

Imperfect Information in Imperfect Competition
Under imperfect competition, producers and consumers usually lack knowledge of the **market, such as prices charged by rival firms, production techniques and**

product quality. Firms may not be aware of the most cost-efficient methods of production or the production processes used by rival firms. Consumers may not be fully aware of product prices and quality.

Imperfect information also serves as a barrier to entry which helps to accord firms some degree of **market power**, giving them a **price-setting ability** (to maintain some degree of control over their price-output combination) due to the downward sloping demand curve. For example, a nasi lemak stall may have created a secret recipe which allows it to differentiate its product from other stalls and charge a higher than usual price. Furthermore, imperfect information provides incentive for firms to engage in **R&D and innovation**, since it may not be easy for other firms to gain enough information about their innovation efforts to duplicate them.

Thus, imperfect information may enable firms to enjoy greater **market dominance**. The greater the firm's market dominance and market power, the more price-inelastic the demand for the good, leading to a greater deadweight welfare loss and a more severe **underallocation of resources** to the production of the good. This exacerbates **market failure**.

Imperfect Information in Persuasive Advertising
Persuasive advertising can contribute to people's ignorance by overselling product benefits, misleading them as to the true benefits of a good. An example would be digitally enhancing photos in cosmetics advertisements. This may lead to consumers overestimating the MPB of the good, leading to overconsumption of the good and a higher than socially optimal level of consumption/production.

Persuasive advertising may also be perceived to be a waste of scarce resources, since resources are spent on advertising, which is perceived to be **non-productive** instead of producing more output. Thus, persuasive advertising may be deemed detrimental to consumer and societal welfare.

Asymmetric Information
In the presence of asymmetric information, one side of the market (producer/consumer) possesses more information than the other side, that is, the information available to both sides of the market differs. For example, in healthcare, the doctor knows more about the patient's health than the patient and may prescribe more tests and treatments than the socially optimal amount in order to earn greater revenue and profits. This would then be a case of **supplier-induced demand**. Due to imperfect information, demand is higher than required, leading to the overconsumption of tests and treatments. This leads to **allocative inefficiency** and **market failure**.

Macro Link:

<u>Imperfect Information in the Job Market</u>
In the labour market, imperfect information means that workers lack perfect knowledge of the job opportunities and wages available. Likewise, firms also lack perfect knowledge of the suitability of workers they have hired and/or whether there are better candidates available. This is one of the main causes of **frictional unemployment**, which is the time period between jobs when workers are searching for jobs or transitioning from one job to another.

Evaluation:

<u>Imperfect Information on the Government's part</u>
The government, too, is not in possession of perfect information. For example, it may over or under-estimate the MEC or MEB of a good, causing them to implement an inappropriate or ineffective level of taxes or subsidies. Imperfect information on the part of the government can lead to **government failure.**

<u>Information Provision and Campaigns</u>
The best way to resolve the problem of imperfect information is to correct it at its source, by educating the public about the real costs and benefits of a good through information provision and campaigns. However, it is often **very difficult to change mindsets** even with the information provided. For example, in the case of smoking, numerous education campaigns have been implemented to raise awareness about the ill effects of smoking, and cigarette packaging usually features graphic warning messages to advise the public against smoking. Yet, smoking is still commonplace due to its addictive nature, which suggests that there is a limit to the effectiveness of such educational campaigns. In addition, such campaigns can be **costly** and their effects are usually only observed in the **long run**.

54. Explain what is a Public Good and its implications.

A **public good** is a good that possesses the 2 key characteristics of **non-excludability** and **non-rivalry** in consumption. Non-provision of public goods is a source of **market failure**.

Non-Excludability
Non-excludability means that once the good has been provided, it is not possible or prohibitively uneconomical to prevent anyone from benefitting from the good, leading to the **free-rider problem** as individuals are able to benefit from the provision of the good without paying for it. As one can consume the good without paying, there is no incentive for any rational consumer to pay for these goods. As a result, it is not profitable for firms to provide the good and the good is simply not provided, leading to the problem of a **missing market** and **complete market failure**.

Non-Rivalry
The benefits of a non-rivalrous good are not depleted by an additional user, that is, the consumption of the good by one person will not reduce the amount of the good available to others. This also implies that the **marginal cost** of providing the good for an additional user is **zero**. Since the allocatively efficient output level occurs where P=MC and now MC=0, this would imply that allocative efficiency occurs at **zero price** (i.e. P=0). As **no rational producer will produce to sell a good at $0**, this simply means that the good will not be produced/consumed at the socially optimal output level when it is provided. There will be underconsumption if the good is provided by the free market, as a positive price will be charged and since MC=0, P>MC and there will be **allocative inefficiency**.

An example of a public good is street lighting. Once it has been provided, it is difficult to exclude anyone in the vicinity from benefitting from the illumination provided. Thus, the street lighting can be said to be **non-excludable**. In addition, any number of people in the vicinity can benefit from its provision; thus, it is also said to be **non-rivalrous** in nature.

Evaluation:

Direct provision
In order to resolve market failure generated by public goods, direct provision of the public goods is required. However, as the government needs to finance the provision of these public goods, direct provision could impose a strain on the government budget. Hence, the government still needs to weigh the costs and benefits of each good provided, rather than providing every public good, as there are opportunity costs to the use of government funds which must be considered. For example, other merit goods may have to be forgone if a public good is provided instead.

Even after deciding to provide the public good, there is still a need to decide on the level of provision. This is not easy to ascertain especially since the market demand is not present as consumers, in a bid to free-ride, do not reveal their true valuation of the good.

Quasi-public good

A quasi-public good is best defined as a good which is **close in nature** to a public good, or a **semi**-public good. For example, digital content and media uploaded on the internet may be **excludable** to some extent (through password encryption, online payment etc.) but there are also many examples of how these can be easily circumvented by hackers, and how practically anyone can easily obtain copies of most digital content. In addition, it is also **non-rivalrous**, since the provision of this content to certain users does not deplete its benefits for another user since downloading a master file does not reduce the amount of downloads available to other users.

Another example would be that of **expressways**. Although they could be, to some extent, **excludable** in nature (via road gantries, tollbooths etc.), it may be economically prohibitive in other circumstances to prevent road users from using expressways once they are provided. In addition, they are usually **rivalrous** in nature during the peak period as many vehicles will be present on the road and each vehicle occupies a certain amount of space on the road, depleting the space available to other vehicles and potentially leading to road congestion. However, during off-peak periods, there may be wide stretches of empty roads which are **non-rivalrous in nature** as one vehicle's presence will not have an effect on the space available to another vehicle.

Such goods may be considered **semi-excludable** and **semi-rivalrous**, and are termed **quasi-public goods.**

55. Explain how Direct Provision works.

Governments may undertake the provision of **public goods** and some **merit goods** with significant positive externalities, with state funding used to finance the direct provision of these goods to the public at a subsidised price (for merit goods) or zero price (for public goods and certain merit goods).

Public Goods
Public goods may be essential to an economy (e.g. street lighting, national defence), yet they are not provided under standard free market mechanisms due to the problems of **non-excludability** and **non-rivalry**. Without government intervention, there would simply be zero provision, possibly leading to a significant deadweight welfare loss to society. Thus, the government can use its tax revenue to finance the development and operation of public goods. It should be noted that due to the problem of non-excludability, the government would also charge **zero price** for consumption of the public good.

For example, in Singapore, the government fully finances the provision of street lighting with its tax revenue and engages contractors such as PowerGrid for maintenance works.

Merit Goods
In the case of merit goods which are significantly underconsumed/produced due to imperfect information, positive externalities or excessive income inequality, the government can choose to directly provide such goods. This is especially the case when the externalities are very significant, and direct provision will help to ensure that adequate supply and adequate consumption will be achieved. However, direct provision does not necessarily mean that the merit good is provided for free. For example, HDB flats are directly provided by the government at a subsidised rate.

Merit goods can be directly provided for three reasons: **Equity**, **positive externalities and imperfect information**.

Equity: The provision of merit goods should not be entirely left to the free market, which allocates goods based on consumers' willingness and ability to pay. Due to the intrinsic desirability of merit goods, they should be made available to all of society, including lower-income households. Thus, direct provision targeted at lower income households helps to ensure a more equitable distribution of merit goods. An example is the Polyclinics in Singapore, which provide primary healthcare mainly to the lower income households.

Positive externalities: In addition, merit goods generate substantial positive externalities which are not taken into account by the free market. This may lead to substantial under-consumption of merit goods which can be resolved through direct provision, which can help to increase the supply, lower the price and increase the consumption of merit goods.

For instance, the direct provision of housing can help to ensure that positive externalities such as increased social stability (as citizens' basic need for shelter is fulfilled), better public health and improved environmental standards are taken into account. Direct provision causes the supply curve of housing to increase and shift rightward as shown in the diagram below, such that at the new free market equilibrium where MPB = SS (with DP), the socially optimal output Qs is achieved.

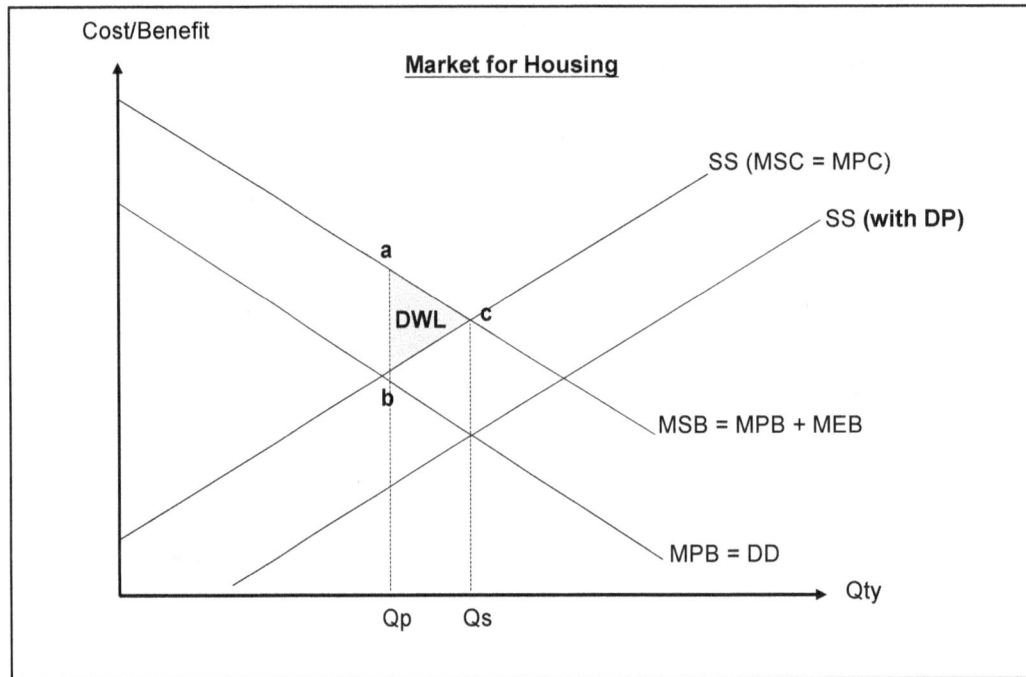

Imperfect information: Direct provision also addresses the underconsumption of goods due to consumer ignorance, by increasing supply, reducing prices and thus encouraging more consumption.

Evaluation:

Joint Production
It is still possible for the government to work together with the private sector to provide merit goods. For example, in Singapore's healthcare sector, the government builds public hospitals (Tan Tock Seng Hospital, KK Women's and Children's Hospital) which serve to complement private hospitals (such as Mount Alvernia Hospital, Gleneagles Hospital etc.) as well as private GP clinics and pharmacists. Both the public and private sector work together to provide the people with the comprehensive healthcare treatments they require.

High Opportunity Cost/Strain on Government Budget
Often, huge funds are required to finance the development and provision of a public

or merit good and this **exerts a strain on the government's budget**. As government expenditure is financed by taxation, heavier taxes may have to be imposed on the public, potentially leading to a disincentive to work and invest. The high opportunity cost of providing public/merit goods also means that less tax revenue is available to spend on other aspects such as social development and fiscal policy.

Imperfect Information

The government may find it difficult to determine the type of public/merit good to provide and in what quantity, as well as to valuate the consumer's demand for the good due to non-revealed consumer preferences pertaining to public goods. In the case of merit goods, the marginal external benefit (**MEB**) of the merit good may also be difficult to determine. A **lack of precision** may lead to an inappropriate (less than/more than socially optimal) amount of the good being produced, and societal welfare is not maximized.

Productive Inefficiency

Due to the lack of incentive to maximize profits, the government may be **productively-inefficient** in its production of the good and operate at higher costs than necessary.

To resolve this problem, the government can corporatise certain entities which have to be financially disciplined and accountable. In the case of Singapore's healthcare, for example, we have MOH Holdings, Singhealth, National Healthcare Group (NHG), and JurongHealth which are owned by the government but are corporatised entities which have to be financially viable.

Greater Deadweight Welfare Loss

Direct provision of a merit good may lead to a **greater deadweight welfare loss** if the good is provided free. In the free market, the good is consumed where MPB = MPC at output Qp, leading to a deadweight welfare loss of area A due to underconsumption of the good. However, if the good is now free, then MPC to consumers is 0 and the new free market equilibrium occurs at the point where MPB = MPC = 0. This may be depicted by a fall in the MPC curve to MPC' (reflecting a full subsidy provided at Q2). This corrects the original underconsumption of healthcare, but leads to overconsumption of healthcare and a new deadweight welfare loss equivalent to area B.

Depending on the relative sizes of areas A and B, direct provision at zero price may or may not lead to a greater deadweight welfare loss for society. If government intervention worsens the extent of the allocative inefficiency, it will be an instance of **government failure**.

The smaller the MEB, the lesser the extent of under-consumption, and the greater the likelihood of government failure. **As such, the government should only provide the merit goods for free if the size of the MEB is very large.**

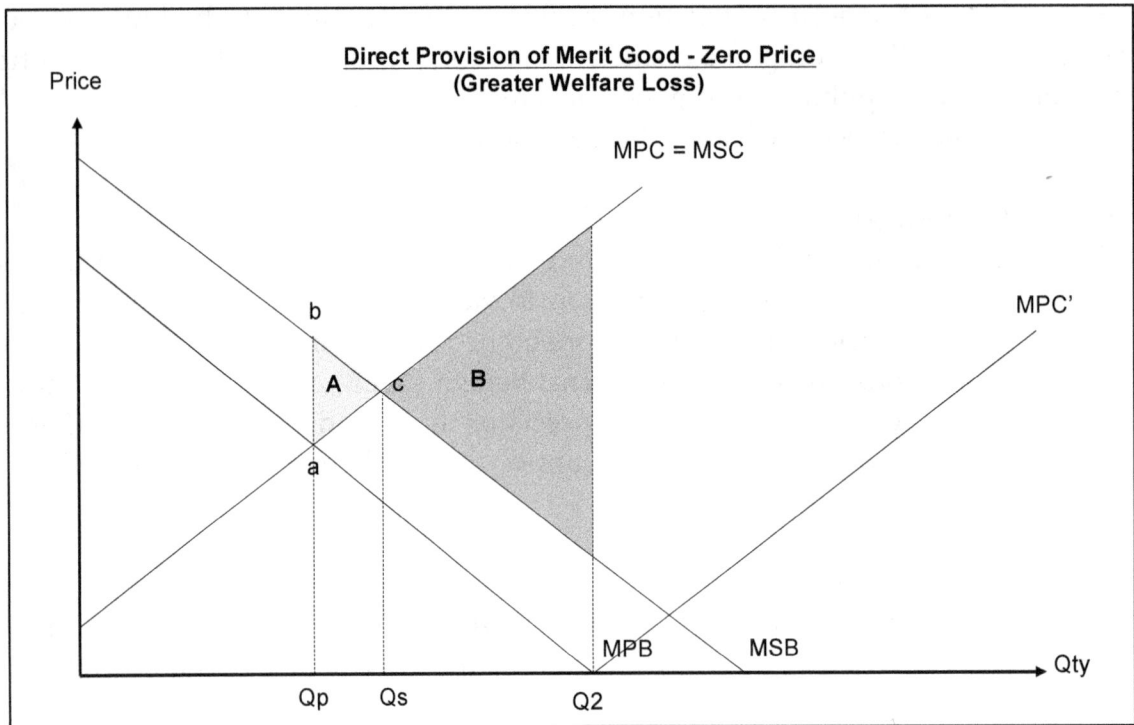

Direct Provision of Merit Good - Zero Price
(Greater Welfare Loss)

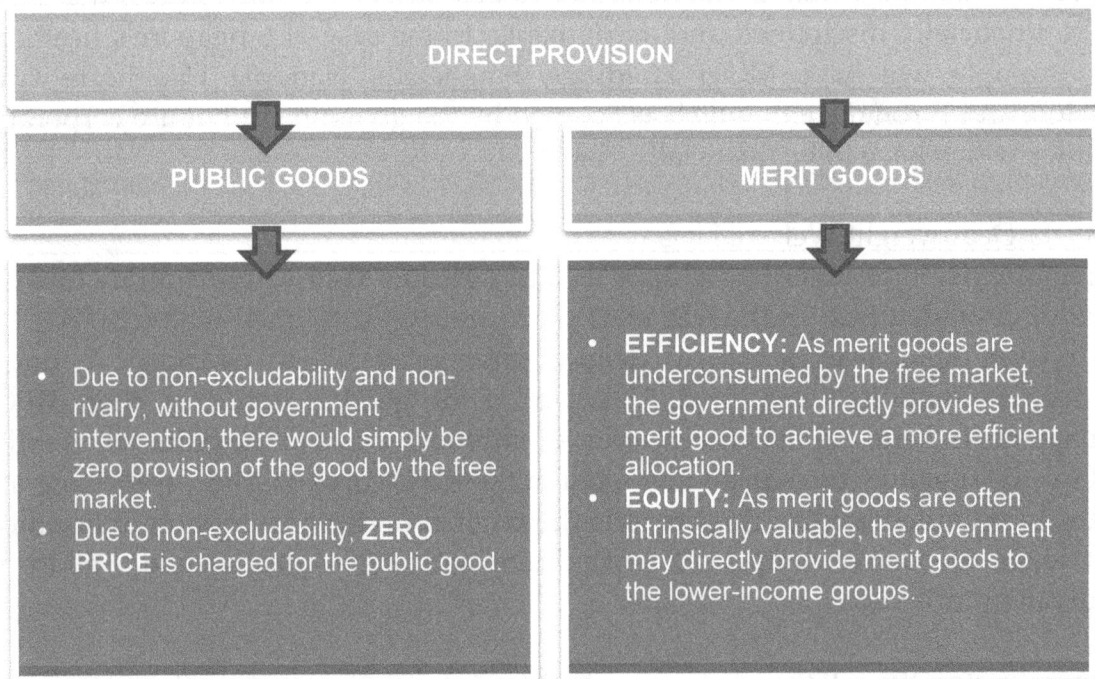

DIRECT PROVISION

PUBLIC GOODS

- Due to non-excludability and non-rivalry, without government intervention, there would simply be zero provision of the good by the free market.
- Due to non-excludability, **ZERO PRICE** is charged for the public good.

MERIT GOODS

- **EFFICIENCY:** As merit goods are underconsumed by the free market, the government directly provides the merit good to achieve a more efficient allocation.
- **EQUITY:** As merit goods are often intrinsically valuable, the government may directly provide merit goods to the lower-income groups.

56. Using an example, explain how a tax works to correct negative externalities.

In order to correct the negative externalities such as **pollution** from the production/consumption of a good, the government can **levy a specific tax which is equivalent to the monetary value of the negative externalities (or MEC)** which is generated per unit of output. In this example, **the tax will compel the polluting firm to internalize the external costs of their production.**

As shown in the diagram below, a specific tax of AB which is equivalent to the MEC raises the firm's cost, shifting its supply curve upwards from **MPC** to **MPC + Tax**, coinciding with the **MSC**. At the new equilibrium where MPB = MPC + Tax, the firm will produce the **socially optimal output Qs** which is where **MSB = MSC**. At this equilibrium, overallocation of resources is corrected as there will no longer be overproduction relative to the socially optimal amount. The tax also eliminates the deadweight welfare loss **ABC** arising from overproduction prior to the imposition of the tax.

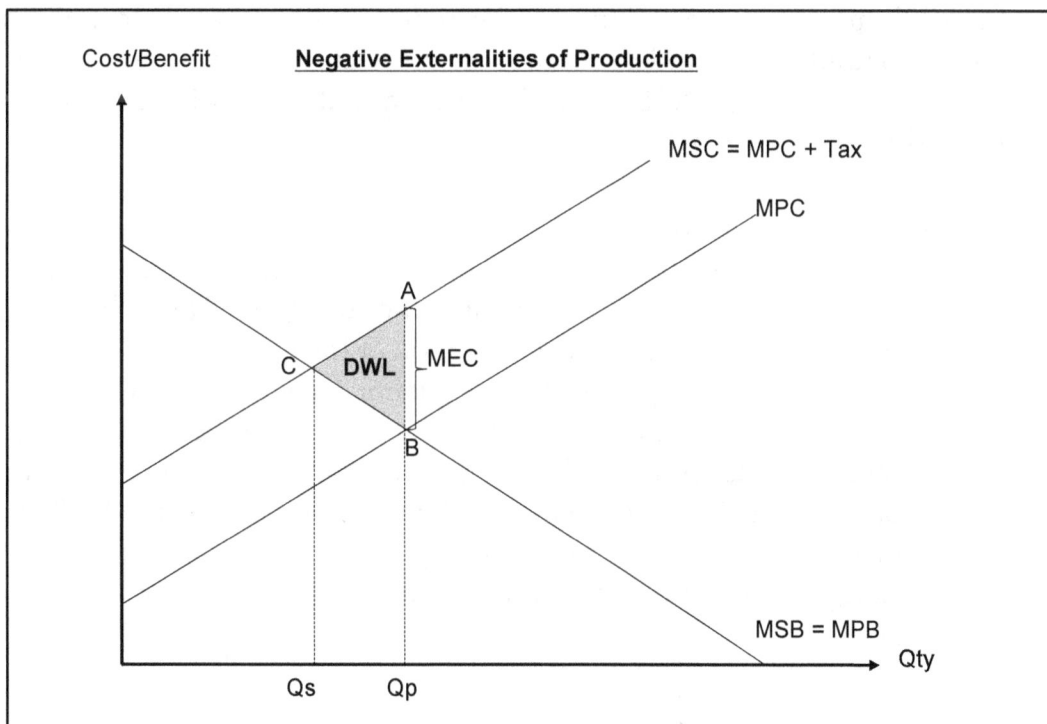

Refer to previous questions (e.g. Question 49) for a full explanation of externalities.

Evaluation:

<u>Merits</u>

- Taxes are fairly **flexible** and can be adjusted according to the MEC value (or the extent of the negative externalities) to achieve a more precise outcome.
- Taxes are a **market-based** policy. Firms are still allowed to pursue self-interest and produce at the point where the **new MPC = MPB**. The imposition of a tax allows the market to continue operating according to market forces to reach a new state of equilibrium. For example, if demand increases, the socially optimal output will also increase, and the market will then automatically adjust such that the new free market equilibrium will also coincide with the new Qs.
- Taxation provides **revenue** for the government to finance the provision of merit and public goods.

<u>Limitations</u>

- Taxation requires **accurate valuation** of the external cost/MEC but in practice, it is difficult to estimate the monetary value of externalities. The overvaluation of the MEC may cause the output to be reduced to a point below the socially optimal output, while undervaluation of the MEC may result in the output not being lowered enough to the socially optimal output. **Societal welfare cannot be maximised with a lack of precision.**
- If the demand for certain goods (such as cigarettes and other addictive/habitually consumed substances) is highly **price-inelastic**, an increase in the price of this good due to the tax will only lead to a less than proportionate fall in the quantity demanded of the good. Thus, the tax may not be effective in lowering the overconsumption of the good.
    - In order to bring down the quantity consumed/produced to the socially optimal level, a **higher tax** will be required. However, **indirect taxes are regressive**, which means that they take up a larger proportion of the lower-income group's income as compared to the higher-income group, reducing their purchasing power to a greater extent. This could exacerbate the problem of **income inequality** in society.

57. Explain how Legislation can work to correct positive externality.

Legislation is defined as the process of controlling business and consumer activities through laws and administrative rules. In the case of goods which generate positive externalities, such as **education**, legislation can help to correct the positive externality through laws and rules such as the **Compulsory Education Act** in Singapore. Under this law, parents who fail to enroll their children in school up to Primary 6 will face penalties such as fines and/or imprisonment.

As shown in the diagram below, making education mandatory has the effect of legislating the amount of consumption to be Qs, with the perfectly inelastic demand curve DD1 representing the legislated amount which ideally coincides with the socially optimal level of consumption/production, **Qs** where **MSB = MSC**. As a result, underallocation of resources is corrected as there will no longer be underconsumption of the good relative to the socially optimal amount. The law also eliminates the deadweight welfare loss **ABC** arising from underconsumption prior to the imposition of the legislation.

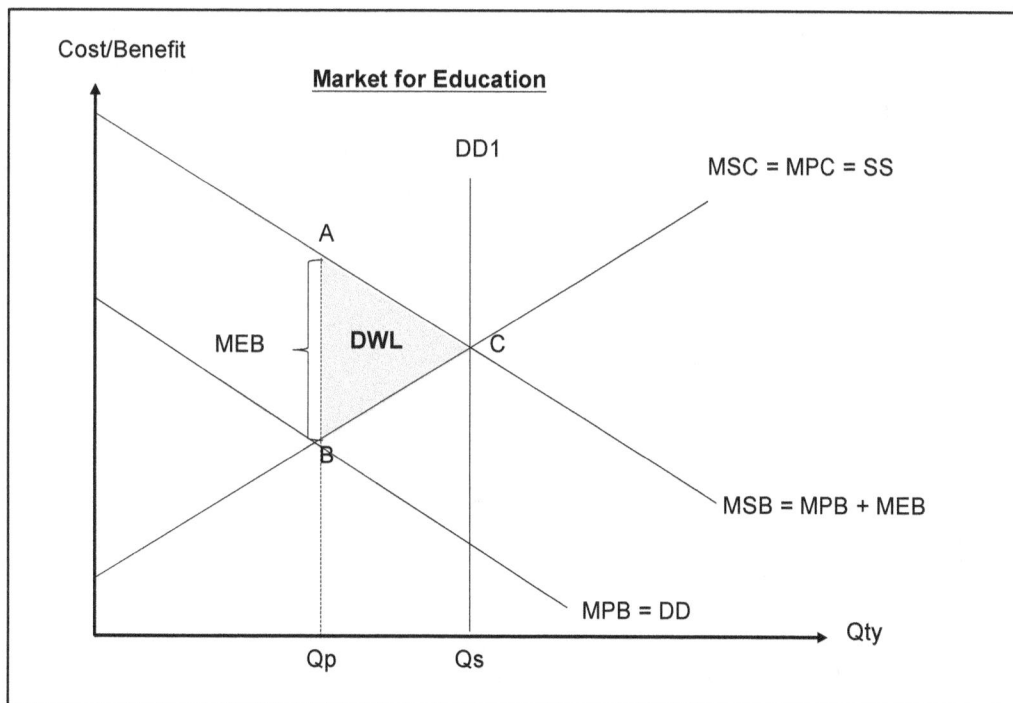

Evaluation:

Merits

- Legislation may be **simpler and more practical** to implement compared to market-based measures such as subsidies to correct positive externalities. It may also be easier to estimate the socially desirable/optimal amount than to estimate the value of the MEB.

- As there is a penalty for breaking the law, regulations compel producers and consumers to comply with existing rules, and **effectively deter** economic agents from producing/consuming at levels they would otherwise choose. Thus, there is a **greater guarantee** that the socially optimal output level can be reached, compared to other policies.

Limitation

- The implementation and enforcement of laws often require **high enforcement and monitoring costs**.
- The government may possess **imperfect information** and may be grossly wrong in its estimation of the socially optimal level of output/production. It is also difficult to estimate the level of penalty for the good, which must be sufficiently harsh to be an effective deterrent.
- Legislation is a **blunt tool** which forces economic agents to comply with fixed rules and regulations, displacing the role of the price mechanism in allocating resources and thus preventing the market from operating according to free market forces. When market forces have changed, legislation does not automatically adjust to the change in the socially optimal level of consumption/production.
- **Equity** may suffer. From the diagram, as demand increases (as dictated by legislation) to D1, price increases. Lower-income households may thus be forced to reduce their consumption of other necessities such as food. As such, legislation is **best accompanied by other measures** such as **subsidies**.

58. Explain how Education campaigns work to address Market Failure pertaining to a demerit good.

Education campaigns can help to correct market failure arising from **imperfect information** by providing more information to allow the real costs/benefits of consumption or production of a good to be made known to the public. In the case of demerit goods, this helps to **decrease the demand for demerit goods** so that the socially optimal amount will be consumed. Examples of education campaigns include brochures and pamphlets informing the public of the ill effects of gambling, health warning messages accompanied by graphic images on cigarette packet packaging, and so on.

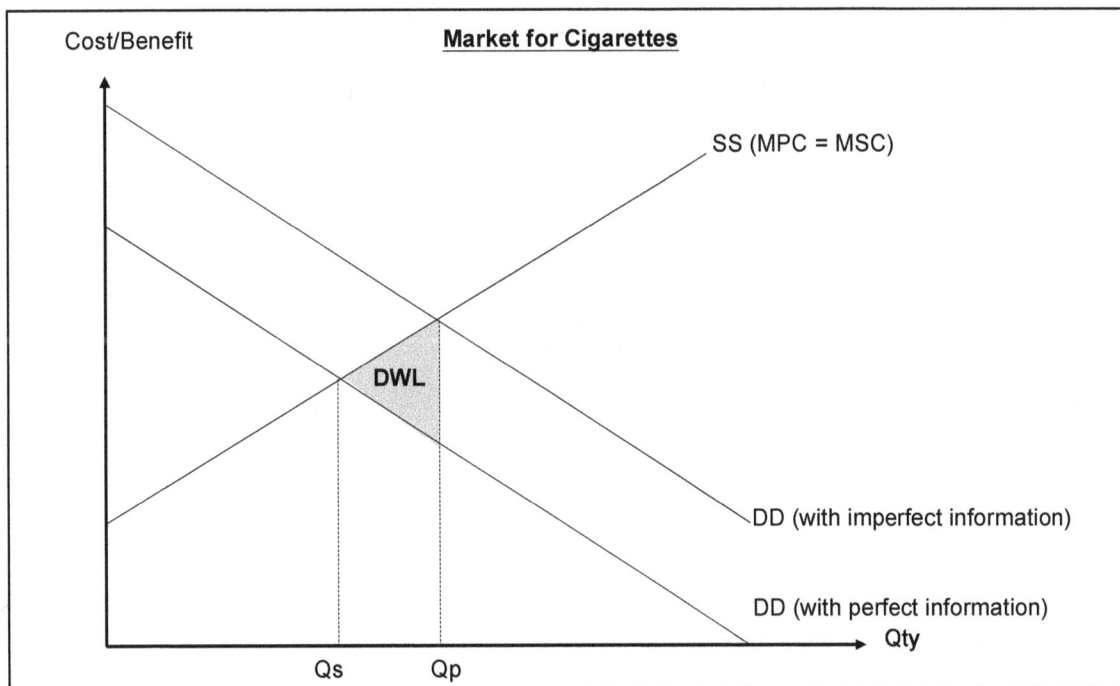

Education campaigns inform consumers of the **real costs** which they will incur from consuming cigarettes, altering their tastes and preferences away from consuming cigarettes, shifting the demand curve downward from **DD (with imperfect information)** to **DD (with perfect information)**. At the new free market equilibrium where DD=SS, the socially optimal output **Qs** is also achieved, thus correcting the overallocation of resources to production/consumption of the demerit good, and eliminating the deadweight welfare loss to society due to allocative inefficiency.

Evaluation:

Merits

- Education campaigns are effective in the long-term in helping to correct market failure caused by imperfect information, as they directly deal with the root cause yet allow consumers/producers to continue to pursue self-interest and consume/produce at the point where MPC = MPB.

<u>Limitations</u>

- **Significant government expenditure** is usually required to fund education campaigns and this can put strain on the government's budget. There is an **opportunity cost** as money could have been better spent on other aspects (e.g. infrastructural development) which could have benefitted society to a greater extent.

- Often, the effects of education campaigns are only seen in the **long run** as time is required for consumers to be educated and to change their consumption patterns. As such, education campaigns should usually be **complemented** by other shorter-term measures (e.g. taxes) to be more effective.

- Mindsets may be very difficult to change, and so the campaigns may turn out to be ineffective despite plenty of time, effort and funds expended.

59. Explain how road widening and road building projects work to reduce congestion.

Road congestion is a negative externality generated by **road usage**, particularly in cities such as Singapore or Bangkok where there is limited land area for road space coupled with a high population density. The **marginal private cost (MPC)** of a car journey includes petrol costs, the carpark charges, the wear and tear of tyres, and the personal time cost of delays. However, the **marginal external cost (MEC)** of a car journey is the delay (time cost) to all other motorists (third parties) who use the same road and encounter congestion (including passengers on public buses). This causes a divergence between the MPC and the marginal social cost (MSC), which is higher, and leads to an overallocation of resources to road/car usage as there are **more cars on a given stretch of road** than is socially optimal.

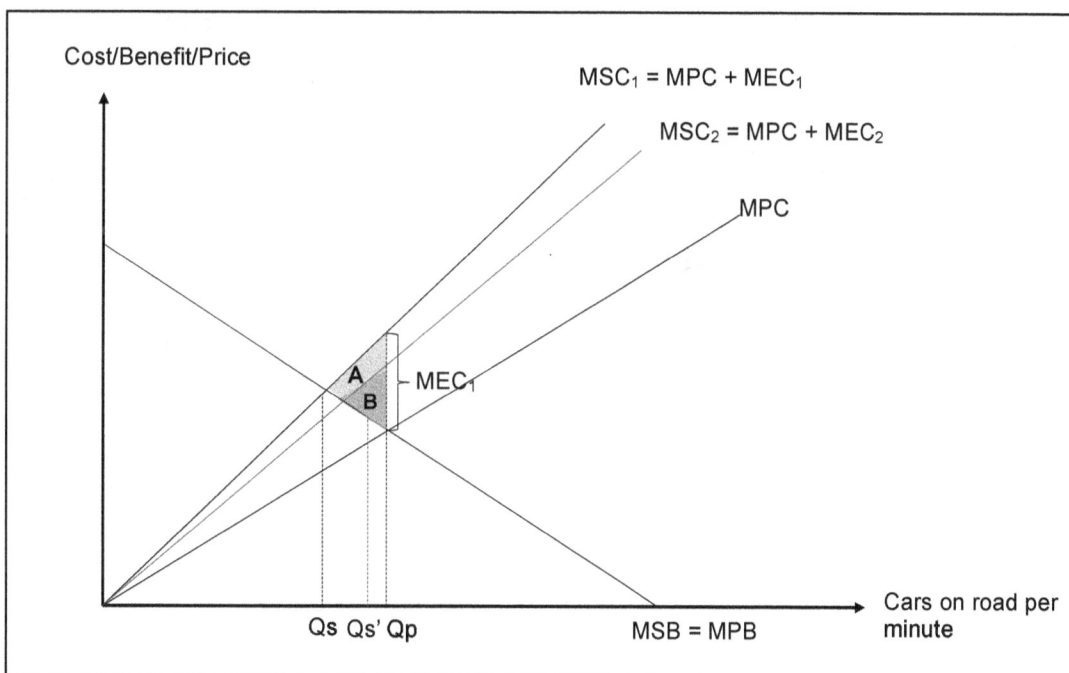

*Note: The MSC curve is reflected as an upwards anti-clockwise pivot of the MPC curve and not just an upward shift. This is because for every car added to the road, the extent of the congestion will increase at an increasing rate since congestion worsens for **all** motorists. Therefore, the MEC increases with more cars on the road.*

Road widening and building can help to reduce congestion by providing alternative routes for cars to travel, or by increasing the optimal number of cars which can travel on the widened road. It helps to decrease congestion without decreasing road/car usage, thus effectively reducing the MEC of a car journey on that road. In other words, it **shifts the MSC curve downward** such that the new socially optimal output (Qs') is now closer to the existing free market equilibrium output (Qp).

This reduces the extent of the overconsumption and causes the deadweight welfare loss to society to decrease from (A+B) to B as shown in the diagram, without having to reduce car/road usage.

Note:

Only such solutions are able to change the **social costs/benefits** and shift the **MSC/MSB** curve. In the context of road congestion, using other measures (such as Electronic Road Pricing or improving public transport) will cause **private costs/benefits** to change, leading to a shift in the **MPB/MPC** curve.

Evaluation:

- Road widening/building can be an ideal long-term solution, which increases societal welfare since the deadweight welfare loss can be decreased without decreasing car usage. This solves the **root problem** of limited road capacity.

- However, it is a **long-term solution** as it takes time to build and widen roads. Moreover, **high expenditure** on the part of the government will be required, which could potentially impose a strain on the government budget.

- In addition, **other externalities** may be generated in the midst of construction, such as pollution.

- There is also an **opportunity cost** in terms of the other purposes for the land, which have to be sacrificed. In the case of **land-scarce** Singapore, the opportunity cost is very high as the amount of land available is **very limited**, but has to be apportioned to many different alternative uses.

60. Explain cap and trade policy.

Tradable permits are **permits to pollute** which are issued to firms by an international body/government and can be traded (bought/sold) in a market. Under a **cap and trade (tradable permit)** system, the total number of permits released into the market is capped at the total amount of pollution, which is deemed acceptable. For example, in the diagram below, the number of permits is capped at **Q1** by the government, and is reflected by a perfectly price-inelastic supply of permits. Each firm is then granted a particular number of credits/permits to discharge a defined quantity of pollutant into the atmosphere over a fixed period of time. The initial assignment of permits is either determined through **auction**, or **distributed freely** to the firms.

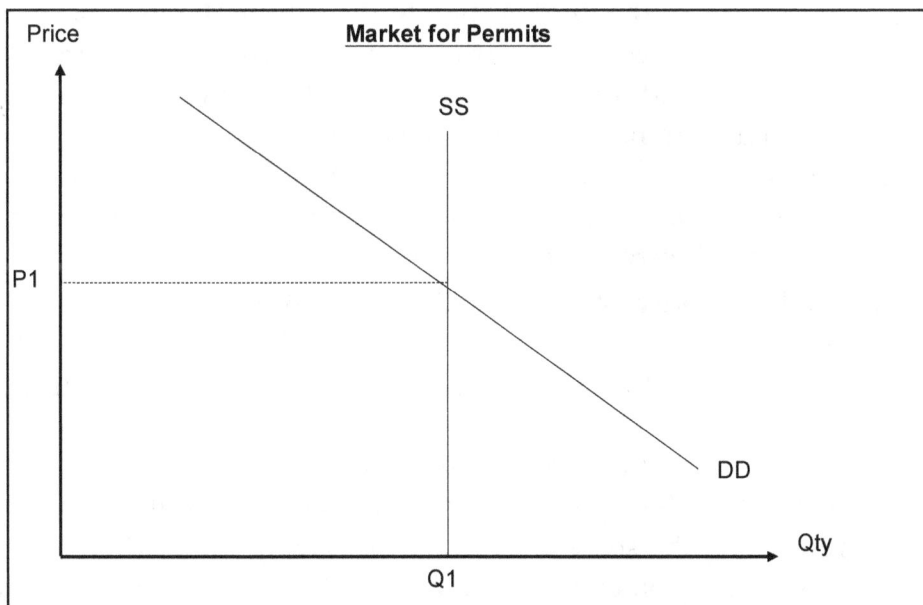

Permits can be **traded** – they can be bought or sold in the market among interested firms, with the price of permits being determined by market conditions of demand and supply. For example, the price of the permits as shown in the diagram above is P1 where DD for permits = SS for permits. If a firm can produce its product by emitting a lower level of pollutants than the level set by its permits, it can **sell its extra permits in the market** for a profit. However, if the firm needs to emit more pollutants than the level set by its permits, it must **buy more permits in the market**, or face heavy penalties.

The decision as to whether a firm should buy or sell permits is dependent on how cheaply the firm can reduce emissions.
- If the cost of reducing pollution is higher than the price of the permit, the firm will choose to buy additional permits and pollute.
- Otherwise, the firm will cut pollution and sell permits in the market until the

cost of reducing pollution = the price of permits.

Evaluation:

Merits:
- Cap and trade policy combines the strengths of the **command and control approach** with **market-based incentives**.
- Assuming the government has enough information, if the **quantity of permits is equal to the quantity of emissions, which is optimal**, then the permit system is effective as the **socially optimal level can be targeted**, and **a reduction in the overall pollution level is guaranteed**.
    - The government can achieve the desired level of emissions much more precisely than taxes and subsidies. **It is easier to set the optimal level of permits in the market than to determine the monetary value of the MEC**, which would have to be determined if taxes were used instead. Under cap and trade, it is the free market forces of demand and supply which determine the price of the permit.
    - The government can **progressively** reduce the number of permits issued to the polluting firms, allowing total pollution in the affected industry to be reduced over time.
- Cap and trade is more **cost-effective** than legislation.
    - Most of the decrease in emissions will be undertaken by firms which are **able to reduce their emissions at the lowest cost**, since they would simply choose to buy permits if the opportunity cost of doing so is less than the cost of reducing emissions.
    - In addition, the system penalizes buyers of permits for polluting, while rewarding the seller of permits for having reduced emissions. If firms can cut back on emissions at a relatively low cost, they can sell permits in the market for a profit. **This allows pollution to be reduced at a lower overall cost to society than using legislation compared to if the government simply forces every firm to decrease pollution.**
- Cap and trade can lead to a **desirable dynamic effect** as it encourages firms to **adopt cleaner technologies** in the long run so that they can sell their excess permits and increase their total revenue. Assuming that firms are profit-maximising, the additional revenue which they can earn from selling their permits offers an **additional incentive** to innovate.
    - Conversely, taxes do not directly incentivise firms to switch to cleaner production methods as the indirect tax is usually based on the firm's **output**, rather than the **amount of emissions** produced by the firm.
    - If firms are able to cut costs using alternative means and offset the loss of profits from the imposition of the indirect tax, they would be able to continue production without reducing their emissions or they could pass on the bulk of the tax burden to consumers if demand for their good was price-inelastic.

Limitations:

- The governing body may face **difficulties in implementation** of the scheme as it may be technically difficult to measure emissions in some cases (e.g. if the source of the pollution is mobile) and to set up a mechanism of monitoring and verifying actual emissions.
    - Cap and trade may not be feasible for some types of externalities such as pollution from cars, which are difficult to measure and monitor.
    - Government may lack sufficient information on the type of pollution and the current/optimal level of pollution to be able to set the permit level. The government may end up providing too many permits and cause the price of the permits to be too low, which will not incentivise any reduction in pollution. This has been the case in Europe, where the European Union Emission Trading Scheme has been criticized for allowing an oversupply of permits which have been largely ineffective in incentivising firms to cut pollution.
- The governing body needs to establish a system which **allows permits to be distributed to polluting firms in a fair manner.**
    - Otherwise, political favouritism may arise as governments might accord preferential treatment to some of their supporters and allocate them a larger number of permits than justified.
- A cap and trade system may serve as a **distraction** to firms, drawing them away from their core business. Instead of focusing on enhancing their productivity and competitiveness, they may now be distracted by the tradeable permit market and focus on profiteering from it instead (i.e. by selling excess permits for a profit).
- The danger of **anticompetitive behaviour** leading to **excessive monopoly power** may arise, as the cap and trade system may be abused by large firms which intentionally hoard permits. This serves as a barrier to entry to new entrants and also poses a threat to competitors, which might not be able to produce without emitting and yet are unable to buy more permits to enter the market. This 'squeezes' rivals out of the market, forcing them to close their firms, and potentially leads to market failure due to excessive monopoly power in the market.
- In countries with a small domestic market (such as Singapore), a cap and trade system may not be effective due to the problem of a **thin market**. For example, in Singapore's oil refining industry, it is difficult to match buyers (of permits) to sellers as there are simply not enough buyers and sellers in the market for trade to take place.
- In order to ensure that firms do not try to cheat the system or attempt to deceive regulators rather than pay for their permits, the **penalties for non-compliance** must be sufficiently harsh. In addition, there will be high **monitoring and enforcement costs** involved.

CAP & TRADE

- **Tradable permits:** Permits to emit a given amount of pollutants into the atmosphere over a fixed period of time, usually issued by government/international body
- Can be bought and/or sold in the market, where price of permits depends on relative demand and supply of permits
- Decision to buy/sell permits depends on how cheaply firms can reduce emissions

MERITS

- Easier to set optimal level of pollution and permits as opposed to determining the MEC
- Cost-effective, as emissions are reduced by firms which can do so at the lowest cost
- Desirable dynamic effect, promotes use of technology to cut emissions

LIMITATIONS

- Monitoring/implementation difficulties
- Requires a method to distribute permits in a fair/equitable manner
- May distract firms from core business
- May lead to anticompetitive behaviour, leading to excessive monopoly power
- Requires fairly large market to be effective
- Penalties must be severe enough to discourage 'cheating'

www.ingramcontent.com/pod-product-compliance
Lightning Source LLC
Chambersburg PA
CBHW080557220326
41599CB00032B/6516